AMERICA
DO YOU SEE
WHAT I SEE?

A POETIC JOURNEY
THROUGH TIME

HARGIS R. SALEEM

authorHOUSE®

AuthorHouse™
1663 Liberty Drive
Bloomington, IN 47403
www.authorhouse.com
Phone: 833-262-8899

Published by AuthorHouse 03/22/2022

ISBN: 978-1-6655-5524-1 (sc)
ISBN: 978-1-6655-5522-7 (hc)
ISBN: 978-1-6655-5523-4 (e)

AMERICA DO YOU SEE WHAT I SEE?

A POETIC JOURNEY THROUGH TIME
(Explicit content)

By Hargis R. Saleem

Deterioration of school buildings   *No voting rights*

Mass killings

The bug lie   *Starvation*

Black deaths (no justice)   *Sexism*   *Rape*

Destruction of Democracy   *Evil mentality*

Corona virus   *Insurrection*

Drive by shootings   *Drugs deaths (legal and illegal)*

Bad education   *unemployment*   *Homeless-ness*

Racism   *Hatred*   *High cost of food and gas*

NRA   *Private owned prisons*

High profits (the rich keep getting richer)

(KNOW YE THE TRUTH AND THE TRUTH WILL SET YOU FREE)
(they say but Will It ??)

CONTENTS

"IN THIS BOOK"
(MOTIVATION)

This book is a poetic journey through time. A journey that has spanned over fifty years.

This book is for those who have witness the sense-less killings of our people...killings that have been justified by laws and the law enforcers of our country.

This book is a voice for the homeless, the jobless, the misunderstood, and for the millions who see America through UN-adjusted bi-focal and rose color glasses.

This book is for those who have witness and experienced the demise of our educational system. For those who boast constantly of their degrees(which on their walls) but can't understand or won't understand the savage destruction of the minds of our children...which in turn will lead to a savage destructive leadership of our future.

This book us for the parents who children have died needlessly in the streets of America, on the fields of battle, and behind the walls of our prisons. For those who have seen the develop, the growth, and the power of drugs(legal and illegal) as it has taken the lives of the rich and famous, the poor, the fortunate and the UN-fortunate.

This book is the 'last call' for the people of America to come together and look at the 'ugly' that lurks in every corner of our society, in the darkness of our streets, and in some of the minds and souls of those who speaks for us.

Information is knowledge
Knowledge (when understood) is power
Power is freedom
We the people must be free

Hargis

ABOUT THE AUTHOR
ME

Got me some papers from the institution (high school)...diddy bopped all summer long.

Never knowing my past, not caring about my future, no pain, no worries, no responsibilities, no nothing...just diddy bopping and diddy bopping.

Then came 'time' and another institution (college). Away from the madness that took away my youth, while I slept in the bed of ignorance... fucking myself with city wide fame (basketball), enjoying the cum that ran down my legs...into my mind...destroying the brain cells of my true self while trying to diddy bop into a world of make believe.

But it was there waiting, smiling, knowing, and watching. It took me by my balls and bounced off the walls of institutions (whispering in my ear)... "I am life, I am hard, I am cold, I am bitter, but I am sweet... because I understand".

When I opened my eyes, I could not see why 'that' I thought I loved (I didn't love any more) and 'that' I thought I understood (I didn't understand any more).

Drifting from day to day, smiling whenever I felt the urge to cry. Accepting defeats with false thoughts and growing old with a false heart. I had become institutionalized and I had no control over myself... so I diddy bopped and diddy bopped.

I tried to dig myself and found my surroundings strange, found my actions strange. I found a new kind of defeat...a defeat that made me victorious in victories that I didn't (knowingly) even participated in. It had me by my balls and couldn't even cry out. It made me wrong and it made do right, it pulled me up and it pulled me down. It made me scream out my angers to the world...for I had become as life: I became hard, I became cold, and I became bitter.

Fortifying my brain with new hopes and new thoughts. Feeling for the first time, the sun rays of knowledge of 'self'. I didn't stop to see if it was myself or yourself...it felt good and I smiled. I wrapped myself up with good thoughts of the past, the present, and the future...OH!!! it felt so good.

Then I heard that whisper and once again I knew...I am life: I have to be hard, I have to be cold, I have to be bitter, but I, also, have to be sweet...because now I understand.

"May the peace and blessings of God be upon you"

Hargis

AMERICA ... AMERICA

America, America, the home of many states ...
    with polluted air and chemically-made food,
and still you brag about being great.
Your dollar has fallen and ... leadership is crawling.
    Hypocrisy is openly displayed.
Your foreign policy is in shambles ... so with lives you take a gamble,
    because you know that it is war that you must wage.

Your politics are slick ... but your Feds put in a trick,
    exposing some more corruption on Capitol Hill,
but since it was Congress that got exposed (the masters of loopholes),
    the whole matter is now been killed.
And within your States ... is one big unit of hate,
    because racism was rooted in your growth.
So, children grow old ... after being told
    that they are better or worse than most.

America, America, so brave, so strong, so right.
    You have infected the earth ... but what makes matters worse
is that you look at it and say, "Oh, what a sight."

Your resources are there ... but you don't care
    because it's money that controls your heart.
Your morality don't fit in ... and it may be a sin,
    depending on if you are white or dark.
You have gone from land to land ... convincing others that you are the
standard of man,
    and that your lifestyle should be adopted right away.
Democracy is your game ... slavery (they both mean the same),
    it gives others hope of freedom someday.

America, America, the land of the brave ...
    your people are yearning to be free,
to enjoy your good, which is misunderstood
    from sea to shining sea.

REFLECTING AT SEA

It is March of '69 … it's a new life I'm trying.
    Currently, I'm in the United States Navy;
we're on our way to Vietnam … I'm working for Uncle Sam,
    riding the waves and reading about Anglea Davis.

This time last year I was in school … shouting "black power" and trying to be cool,
    but the south had no place for me.
My basketball skills had faded … wasn't doing very good with grades,
    and Chatt. Town was too boring; I had to flee.

There was nothing but foundries and shit … that was trying to make me submit,
    to be like my father and others.
I didn't want to live in this town … so I had an attitude and a frown.
    I had to do some different things in order to go a little further.

I'm somewhat adventuresome, I guess … I joined the Navy and came out West
    where every day is a different thrill.
There were people in the streets having sex … I scream, "What the heck?"
    They told me this is the way hippies lived.

They thought I was insane … cause I looked at them kind of strange
    and said, "I've never seen nothing like this."
People just smiled and walked on by … no one seemed shocked or shy;
    they were having fun, but they smelled like piss.

On this ship (the *USS Buck*), I'm fairly new … I don't know most of the crew,
    but this ship is getting smaller every day.
We're on our way to kill … just to give President Nixon a thrill.
    I think we all need to pray.

A Vietcong, I've never seen ... the news media say they are mean,
      and their lives we've got to go and take.
We'll be shooting day and night ... killing everything in sight.
      I keep hearing that America's freedom is at stake.

Malcolm and Martin said this war is killing mostly blacks ...
Ali said, "Hell no, I won't go," and then he stepped back.
      The government took away his belt.
A lot of blacks seemed pleased ... to see Ali knocked to his knees;
      not even the so-called black leaders came forth to help.

Last year they killed King ... everyone cried and screamed,
      but look at all the blacks that have been killed in this war.
In Alabama, they are letting blacks out of jail ... if they choose to fight
in this hell.
      Black men in America are treated like toys.

I have to bring this poem to an end ... I hope you enjoyed it my friend.
      I just pray that I make it back home.
I've heard that is land is filled with Gold ... that America wants to control.
      All this death for earth to be owned.

CAPITALISM
(IT WILL)

It will keep you poor ... turning your woman into a whore
    by moving faster than your sense of time.
It will drive you insane ... using many different games,
    and have you thinking that everything is fine.

It will give you thoughts of hope ... squeezing by the throat,
    fucking you from sun up to sun down.
It has turned many into slaves ... and more into early graves,
    but still many think it's the best around.

It will have you working eight hours a day ... because to live you have to pay,
    and make you think that you have control of your life.
It will have you so confused ... thinking you can't lose,
    while stabbing you in the back with a knife.

It has this master plan ... that says it's OK to be a man,
    even though you was a woman at birth.
It will have "cum" running from your brain ... hipping you to the game
    as you exploit old mother earth.

It will test your will, your ability, and your skills,
    because money is what flows through its veins.
It will put your mind in a state ... and have you preaching hate,
    trying to exploit some poor-ass lame.

It will never show its true hand ... because the masses will take a stand,
    and remove it from the earth in just one day.
It is deceptive in its look ... making it hard to spot the crooks.
    I'm talking about the capitalist way.

You see, each other we fight ... day and night,
        thinking that our problems were brought on ourself,
but this capitalistic mind ... feeds off crime
        and is protected and controlled by those with wealth.

This system is vicious as hell ... and will cause you to fail,
        because the masses of the people can't see.
But there are a few that are wise, trying to open eyes,
        because they know that We the People must be free.

A MEETING OF THE MINDS

From around the world they came ... to create new games,
    because the leaders are in dismay.
They talked about their disbelief ... over the world's anger and grief,
    and the destruction that's in their way.

England is raising hell ... because of her slavery tales,
    she refuses to give up power anywhere.
The Irish won't quit ... and Argentineans are calling it bullshit,
    because they want control of their own welfare.

In America, what can you say ... anything, anytime, any way,
    because she is the modern-day Babylon,
Crime is sky high ... and for a few dollars, anyone can die;
    confusion is mounting by the ton.

The poor are joined ... by the middle-class income,
    because things have really gotten out of hand.
Factories are shutting down ... no jobs for the blacks or the browns;
    this dollar is forcing everyone to take a stand.

The Middle East is about to explode ... that's the way the story is told,
    because everyone is afraid to live in peace,
but the main reason is that soil ... it is rich with oil,
    so the rumors of war will never cease.

Russia is inserting her will ... through various forceful deals,
    because world balance is the demand of the day.
Poland doesn't understand ... nor does Afghanistan,
    the destruction of the capitalist way.

In Africa, everyone has stolen ... her resources like diamonds and gold,
    and they have spread her people all over the earth.
They made Africa an issue ... that keeps the rich ... richer,
    and her people everywhere are treated the worst.

Iran is at war ... internal and afar,
     because liberation is not an easy pill to swallow,
for those who don't know ... and aren't trying to grow
     don't understand the power of the dollar.

Now a conference is being held ... by all the wardens of all the jails.
     A meeting of the minds is what it is called.
Their goal plain...another game, another name,
     but this destruction will not be stalled.

A meeting of the minds, a meeting of the minds,
     a meeting of the minds is what it is called,
but the meeting of these minds ... the meeting of these minds
     is the reason why this system has got to fall.

FALL OF 2001
(9/11)

America is on the alert,
    explaining lies … trying to build up pride,
and cleaning up all the so-called dirt.

November of this year … everyone was living in fear,
    because of the attack that took place two months ago.
We have a fear of opening the mail … won't fly or ride the rail,
    and that hate within is starting to grow.

We are now bombing another land … killing thousands searching for
one man,
    because Jr. Bush promised that justice will prevail.
The Christian spies are back home … singing praises and happy songs,
    saying that Jr. Bush and God delivered them from hell.

The whole country has gone insane … pushing this hero game.
    I'm talking about the police and firemen that died when the
    buildings can
    down,
but, shit, there are thousands who will breath no more … but their
names won't sell
T-shirts at the store.
    Capitalism—the best hustle around.

So what is the truth about this and that … who really invented and
released that Amtrak
    that got everyone afraid to open up their mail,
and what about that breaded man named Ben … the trainer of terrorists
and Sr. Bush's friend?
    Is he really responsible for making life in America hell?

What is the truth behind the September 11 demise ... that has everyone with crying eyes?

How could this happen to the land of the free?
The CIA knew ... but they only told a few;

that didn't include the ones that will no longer be.

Oh, how soon we forget ... about all of the other shit

that's deeply rooted in this land I which we live.
It's a new way of making a buck ... off the poor—who gives a fuck?

Money is the power in this country ... *still*.

Look at the election that got Jr. Bush his job ... many black votes didn't count, so who really got robbed?

The people, the Country, or Gore—
thousands of jobs have gone away ... since that great and dreadful day.

It makes you wonder who is really minding the store.

So take this information to heart ... and don't be left out in the dark.

Time is moving too fast to try to slow your roll,
so upgrade your hustle and your game ... get that knowledge, don't be ashamed,

because the rules are still made by he who has the gold.

"THE MARK OF THE BEAST"

A mad man is on the loose...with power in his hand to boost
   his goal is to dominate this land we call earth,
the whole world is waiting to see..if this madness going to yell to some reality
   because a war on this planet will make matters worst.

"Weapons of Mass Destruction" is the language of today
   who got them and why...we all need to pray,
that God will intervene...if he so be
   because this leader is so evil...everyone will soon see.

He stole the election and millions of jobs
   now he is trying to steal the planet, with tactics like the mob.
Fuck the U.N. and their purpose in life
   fuck France and Germany and all of their advise.
Fuck the mothers and fathers who children might die
   fuck the news and radio reporters who ask the questions 'why'.
Jr. Bush is the one, this has to be said
   he will lie to you and smile, because of the '666' on his forehead.

The jobless, the homeless, and the ones that are starving today
   can't understand the billions paid to Turkey, just to use their pathway.
Oh people of America, when are we going to see
   the reality of this mentality...it's killing you and me.
Let us unite our efforts together...be you white, black, yellow, or mex
   lets hold up the battle ships and bring back the jets.

This war is not about democracy or freeing the people of Iraq
   it's about 'oil' for the rich and keeping their bank rolls fat.
It's about the shame his father suffered, back in Desert Storm
   it's about the bully been the bully, because up to his ass he is armed.

It's about the rallying of the stock market (the poor has nothing to do
with that)
        it's about covering up his managing of the country, those skills
        he totally lack.

His people are the on television...everyday and every night
        trying to convince the America people, that we must have this fight.
Fighting for world power ain't the same as fighting for peace
        this war won't end with Saddam, because Jr. Bush has the 'mark
        of the beast'.argis3/11/03

"COUNT DOWN"

March of 'oh three'...the world is waiting to see
      if the call of war will be put into play,
Jr. Bush made his call...after forty eight hours, the hammer will fall.
      He told Saddam and his sons they can't stay

The people of Iraq have made it clear...that they are prepared to die here
      in that desert sands they call home,
but Jr. Bush don't give a shit...his 'weapons of mass destruction' is still
gonna hit
      and wipe out Baghdad (right or wrong).

He dropped bombs off his brother's state...to pre-warn Saddam of his fate
      the world knows...'this war'...Iraq can't win,
war ain't no joke...but to Jr. Bush, it's like dope
      the man's heart is filled with sin.

I guess that's not a nice thing to say...about our President today
      but how can he determine who should rule their land,
the Iraqis didn't ask for our aid...but the fat cats of America have got
to get paid
      I'm talking about that 'oil' in that desert sands.

If we take a lesson from the past...Viet Nam wasn't suppose to last
      no ten, twelve, or thirteen years,
but will power is stronger than machines...something we over looked
(it seems)
      to die for their cause and their home, they have no fears.

God rules all things...the mind, the body, and the machines
      and things done in the dark will surely come to light,
aggression is bad...and what makes it sad
      is when men run out of words, they have to fight.

So the world is waiting to see...if Saddam and his sons are going to flee
because Jr. Bush has got destruction on his mind,
if they move on or just sit...Jr. Bush don't give a shit
thousand of people are going to die 'this time'.

Hargis
3/18/03

"USE TO BE"

Things are changing...are changing...things are really changing
    Men are changing into women
    Women are changing into men
    And all of our religious leaders are changing from 'sin to sin'.

Things are changing...
    Use to 'Liquor', then there was 'Smack'
    Use to be 'Weed', then there was 'Crack'
    Use to be 'Ex-ta-SE' but that brought about many deaths
    Use to be 'Cocane' now it's 'Meth'.

Things are changing...
    Use to be a rich land filled with the very poor
    Use to be New Orleans, but it's no more
    But God is still the master of all the things we know
    Evacuating to other cities, he'll just send some mo
    Same sex marriage in the land of the brave
    War in the Middle East sending mothers' young sons to their grave
    The President says "whole on, a new day is near"
    He, also, is talking about terrorism, keeping the people in fear.

Things are changing...are changing...things are really changing
    Use to be called 'the man' because of all of your insights
    Use to be a black man, now you are white
    Use to stand up for your people (back in the day)
    But that 'Government check' got you looking the other way
    Use to be proud of the work you would do
    You, also, use to think that this Government wasn't telling the truth.

Things _are_ changing
    Look at the mentality if our children, they are killing at an early age
    No conscious, no heart, and don't care about jail or the grave
    Technology virus humanity, that the war of today

Trying to get more and more dollars...the American way
Creativity is gone and programs are now set
Their targets are our children,,,who hasn't been born yet
It's hard been broke, in a world where money is king
Use to be love and unity...but now it's back to 'just a dream'.

Hargis
9/21/05

YEAR END "2005"
THE WHOLE WORLD IS NOW WATCHING

Plans are falling from the sky...the people are asking the question 'why'
    when you look at the technology that we have today,
the answer is in the mind...it can't move forward (it has run out of time)
    the mentality of this world, it can not stay.

We've had tornadoes and hurricanes, transplants and a President with
no shame
    that have plagued our country all year long,
we've had thousands killed in Iraq...trying to keep the 'oil kings' fat
    now the people are telling Bush that he was wrong.

Millions of people have been displaced...'F.E.M.A.' was moving slow
because of their race
    it seems like no one has learned from history at all,
racism is running ramped in the 'Land down under'...explosions in
Europe got the people wondering
    is this the beginning of our down fall?

AIDS in Africa is out of control...gangs in America (there membership
grows)
    a strike has shut down New York City,
America people homes are now been bugged...by the President and his
legal thugs
    America, America you are looking kind of 'shitty'.

But many still boast about it's greatness and it's wealth...
about the beauty of the cities that will take away your breath.

We've got diseased in chickens, the cows have gone mad
    now the birds got some shit that's gonna make everybody mad.
They are still looking for Ben Laden...Saddam is now on trial
    cribs' leader 'William' just got fried, even though he changed
    his life style.

Whole families are been killed because the money or the pussy ain't right
  children are still been raped by Priests with their minds uptight.
Unemployment is on the rise and so is gas
  60% of all crimes (in most cities) are committed by those with
  a badge.
Everyone is applying pressure because of that dollar bill
  for those of you reading and listening...this shit us for real.

THE WHOLE WORLD IS WATCHING

Hargis
12/29/05

"PEOPLE OF AMERICA"

Two thousand and six...ain't that a bitch
    I'm back on the scene with a new poem,
the shit done got rough...Korea is calling Jr. Bush bluff
    now everyone is re-upping with new arms.

Jr. Bush is so bad...he's telling everyone to kiss his ass
    he even declared 'Pluto' is too small to be a planet,
he has got Condalissa giving 'head' for votes...his Ambassador of hope
    and setting up sanctions, if she so granted.

His entire six years...has played on the peoples' fears
    by pushing nothing but war and death,
we've lost millions of jobs...there are families that are starved
    but everyone still boast about Americas' wealth.

His second in charge...is a man with no heart
    he shot his only friend in the face,
Iraq is still killing...because Jr. Bush is still willing
    to keep our people in that dangerous place.

Saddam, they say has to be hanged...but was he really the blame
    for the '911 Attack' on our land?,
how many more mothers have to cry...without knowing the answer to why?
    After five years, what ever happened to that Ben-Laden man?

Preachers are still turning children into fags...Congressmen are still
fucking pages (ain't that sad)
    two thousand and six, 'OH WHAT A YEAR',
record numbers turn out to vote...looking for a change and some hope
    but everywhere they turn, Jr. Bush is pushing fear.

Planes are falling from the sky...gangs are doing more drive-by(s)
      schools are falling apart in every state,
the homeless rate has doubled...America can't you see the trouble?
      Just look at those who teach, they are filled with hate.

Our investments are being n taken...our confidence is shaken
      but we now have more Billionaires than we ever had,
commercials are telling you to buy...Corporations profits have reached
a new high
      and still there are people starving (ain't that sad).

They say our minimum wage is going to increase...to another minimum
wage (when is this going to cease?)
      hey, they know that poor can only produce poor,
you work hard all week...it's that pay check you seek
      but after taxes, you realize that you are just a whore.

People of America 'please' try to understand...that there are serious
problems all across this land
      and deception has got most of us turned around,
some try to deal with issues...but this Government is vicious
      it works 24/7 to keep us down.

I told you in a poem way back when...that Jr. Bush was filled with sin
      now he is trying to spread this war to other lands,
he doesn't give a shit about the peoples' will...this man just want to kill
      people of America, we have got to take a stand.

I'm not saying that it's easy (don't get me wrong)...because they will take
your life (if you are not strong).
      But the Constitution gives us the right to make a change,
you have dig deep down in your soul...to take back your 'thinking' control
      to stand up for the truth, and don't be afraid or ashamed.

Hargis
10/13/06

"RECALLS"

Recalls, Recalls...these products aren't right,
  but they are rushed to the consumers cause the money is getting tight.

They make millions before they recall...then apology to you and me,
  hoping that our ignorance and TV are keeping us blind to the reality.

They've recalled chicken and beef...peanut butter and fudge,
  they've recalled cars and toys...lipstick and drugs.

A lot of these recalls items come from China, Korea, and places like Bancock,
  unemployment is high in America...this shit has got to stop.

The Japanese are running Ford and GM out of business...cause profit
governs their success
  we are so depended on other countries...how did we get into
  this mess?

So now 'automation' leads to 'lay off'...putting American jobs at risk,
  there are no recalls for job skills...people of America, do you
  understand this?

It seems like nothing is made in America...but misunderstanding and
bullshit,
  even that would be recalled...if it was on a DVD disc.

Last month they recalled some salad...talking about E-COLi and what
it will do,
  then there were toys with too much lead...(made in China) still
  no jobs for you.

Eighty percent of all of our fish comes from outside of the US.
  With sixty percent of it been real bad...but the "FDA" doesn't
  even test.

Americans are getting sicker and sicker everyday...because recalls come too late,

> when was the last tine you checked the ingredients of the food on your plate?

Some of these products are causing 'birth defects'...wiping out a generation of free thinking beings

> but Corporations have so skillfully maneuvered our emotions, most of us can't see it as a sin.

In the 'Humanity War' of the world...America has dropped the ball,

> cheap labor and more profit is their language, along with the new weapon (recall).

Hargis
11/8/07

"PEOPLE TO PEOPLE"

People to people what does this mean?
>   Some are trying to live the 'American dream'
>   Some are trying to just make ends meet
>   Some are trying to be strong, when they know they are weak.
>   Some are happy just been alive
>   Some walk the streets and talk a whole lot of jive.
>   Some have lives that are spinning with confusion
>   Some wake up every morning in a state of illusion.

People to people what are you saying?
>   That there are some serious problems all across this land.
>   That some relationships are bad because of how we think
>   That the 'FDA' don't care what's in our food or drink.
>   That gun fire in schools and churches are taking people lives
>   That children are playing with matches and causing serious fires.
>   That Coal Mines are unsafe but people have to work
>   That Congress is still passing laws that makes matter worst.

People to people what can we do?
>   Make sure that the person you vote for, promises come true.
>   Make sure you've got a good understanding of your everyday life
>   Make sure you commit to your vows to your husband or your wife.
>   Make sure you teach your children and don't leave it to others
>   Make sure you show your love to your father and your mother.
>   Make sure you take care of your family and your business too
>   Make sure you never forget that "God" is watching you.

Hargis
2/10/2008

"HAVE YOU SEEN?"

Have you seen..
    the brother who calls himself a priest
    who preach and preach, but practice it the least.

Have you seen…
    the long lines of people looking for a job
    and the millions in this country that we know will starve.

Have you seen…
    the 'ugly' that strolls through the streets at will
    ejecting fear into the community, always looking to kill.

Have you seen…
    the homeless…their numbers are growing fast
    no shelters, no food because our society worship "cash".

Have you seen…
    the children who haven't had time to grow
    they're just babies having babies with no directions to go.

Have you seem…
    the drugs they are pouring into our streets
    young kids are looking old, adults have that look of defeat.

Have you seen…
    the break up of our family all across this land
    mothers not teaching their children and fathers not being the man.

Have you seen…
    the same sex marriage, approved in many States
    where are the principles of Christianity and those who claims
    to have faith?.

Have you seen...
  the destruction of the people minds and their wills
  they have made 'money' their God, and for it they will kill.

Have you seen...
  the education of our people?

Have you seen...
  the education of our people?

Have you seen...

Have you?

Hargis
6/16/09

"NO LIES"

In January of 2009...white folks went out of their minds
       because 'blackness' was in the 'white' house at last,
southern whites went in sane...because the President had a Muslim name
       that 'old' racism came to the front fast.

People seems to forget...that all of this shit
       was caused by Jr. Bush,
for eight years...all he preached was fears
       there was nothing economically he pushed.

Now the con-game was on...the 'bail-out' hustle was just about grown
       that 'package' was dropped into Obamas' lap,
a lot of Americans didn't give a shit...this was one man they all wanted to hit
       so they brought forth their best to see if he would snap.

Over the years he was blamed...for all of the heat and too much rain
       and for the hurricanes and tornadoes that tore up this land,
the war was five years old...when he took control
       but he did kill that Ben Linden man.

Republicans got this itch...and S. Palin (the Congressional bitch)
       have summoned up a group for 2012,
their campaign will be Obama and his will...health care, the budget, and
the life style on Capital Hill
       the Republican politicians are set on raising hell.

The stock markets are down and up...the housing situation is still stuck
       and nobody gives a fuck about the poor,
most of us can't hardly eat...some die yearly because of no air or heat
       and the 'homeless' numbers are beginning to sore.

Nothing in this poem is new...to the knowledgeable few
   the political system is still the same,
in the house, 'some' control all the seats...and 'some' take <u>specical interest</u>
<u>money</u> as a treat
   so who do you want to blame?

The rich don't pay tax...to IRS and that's a fact
   and most of the world think they are wise,
   they change the rules everyday...so they can continue to get that pay
   the stuff in this poem are "<u>no</u> LIES".

Hargis
6/11/2011

THE WEATHER REPORT
(MOTHER NATURE IS PISSED)

You work hard all day...seeking that pay
      cause bills and things have got to be paid
the weather is so hot...you just got to stop
      cause all of you energy seems to fade.
Augusts' weather in this city...is like an 'old' lady's titty
      it's dry and just sort of hang,
Now I'm not trying to show any disrespect...I'm just showing the affect
      how the weather bring about a lot of pain.

On the coast, Irene is kicking ass...millions are making changes fast
      cause the wind and rain are getting ready to roll,
she is a category 4...a hurricane whore
      ready to tare up some shit, I am told.
She is bringing waves of over 12 feet...this won't be no treat
      and winds up to 120 miles,
what can humans do...against Mother Nature and her crew?
      Irene is going to move up the coast in style.

In Texas, the heat is bad...50 straight days, the people are mad
      Governor Perry has asked everyone to pray,
you know the heat is no joke...it will suck the life right out of folks
      but God don't like Texas (what can I say).
In DC, everyone is doing the 'snake'...behind the first Washington Quake
      Mother Nature ain't bull shitting this year,
some say America us blessed...but this weather is putting her to a test
      bringing about death, destruction, and fear.

When your day ends...and you are looking for a place to mend
      you know a cool...quiet...spot,
but this heat ain't playing...it's kicking ass all across this land
      you start sweating just walking to the parking lot.

I jump in my car...don't live too far
      don't have enough gas to turn on the air
I see people on the streets...walking in all this heat
      when I roll by they just stare.
So in August of this year...we all should have some fear
      of strokes and heart attacks,
from the ground to the sky...this heat feels like fire
      it's Mother Nature doing her thing, and that's a fact.

Hargis
8/25/11

OH SAY...CAN'T YOU SEE?

There were some people that got killed...in a military drill
      their plane was blown from the sky,
thirty people they say...have seen their last day
      now their families and friends can do nothing but cry.

In another part of the world...a gunman killed men, women, boys, and girls
      he said "it was in the name of Christ",
a Muslim talked about his God...and was beaten by a mob
      they said "they feared for their life".

A mother drowned four of her kids.. and said "that God approved of
what she did"
      then the State allowed her to adopted more,
in 'sippi' no one even hollered...when two little black girls was put in
jail for stealing twelve dollars
      they got "LIFE" because they were black and poor.

Then there was the case where a baby was drown...duck taped and
missing thirty days before found
      the mother was only found guilty for telling a lie,
when they let her go...most people shouted "NO NO NO"
      black folks who watched just said "oh my".

The Government allowed some States...to exercise their hate
      with laws to put and keep Mexicans out,
but they are letting men marry men...ain't that a sin?
      So what is being an American all about?.

Preachers and priests are still doing their thang...taking advantage of
women and little children (oh what a shame)
      all because of an education that won't let them see,
beyond paying bills..and hustling for a meal
      this pressure (called life) just won't let you be.

They gave Vic time for some dogs...a mother drown her baby 'get nothing at all'
　　I guess 'the dog' is mans' best friend,
Madoff took billions in cash...then told the world to kiss his ass
　　　　now he is living a luxurious life in the pen.

A Congress woman got shot in the head...and was left in the store for dead
　　　　everyday people cried and prayed,
but six other people were slang...no one even know their names
　　　　with them, the Capitalist can't get paid.

The stock market is falling like rain...the rich are going insane
　　　　two thousand interviewed for ten jobs this week,
the wealthy sit back and laugh...while their profit grow fast
　　　　people die everyday cause they can't eat.

In England, Africa, and Asia too...people are protesting against being controlled by a few
　　　　the world news is asking the leadership to step down,
the United Nation have gotten involved...bum rushing other countries like the mob
　　　　and the Humanitarians of the world ain't made a sound.

Where are the preachers of peace...and the world police?
　　　　I guess all truths won't see you free,
so the question is still the same...who do you blame?
　　　　For an education that won't let you see.

Hargis
8/19/11

"THE SPEECH"
SEPT. 8, 2011

I saw the President and heard his speech
about jobs that millions of Americans seek.

He laid out a plan about how this thing can work
still, there are millions of unemployed Americans who think he is jerk.

Being black in America, ain't nothing changed
not the clothes, not the language, not even the game.

There are some that will destroy everything in this land
before that will take the advise of a black man.

President Obama is the first but many more are on their way
he is just a blue print that God had to lay.

During the President speech, many Congressmen didn't clap
like 'the speaker of the House', John McCain, and that woman that
looked like crap

He said lets put politics a side and work for the peoples' affections
because 14 millions unemployed Americans can't wait until the next
election.

The President has been fighting for four long years
through racism and injustice while holding back the tears.

If it was me, my speech would have started with "kiss my ass y'all"
I'm talking to Perry, Palin, and that old fucker name Paul.

Like Jackie Robinson, the President has got to be a nan of great strength
because he kicking down doors and uprooting the fence.

White people all over America are showing their true color
they did the same thing (back in the day) to Jesus and a few others.

The Republicans will never support Obama...just because he is black
they sill send everyone through hell, before they will let him come back.

In his speech, he talked about challenging the world
by building new schools and new technology for our boys and girls.

He, also, talked about things that should be M. I. A. (made in America)
right now Mexico, Japan, and China make everything to this day.

He talked about the incentives for business that come back home
and rewards for hiring a person who has been unemployed for so long.

He said lets do right by our veterans and show them some love
giving up their lives for our freedom, they need more than just hugs.

The President told Congress, these things have to be passed
then he looked right into the camera as if to say "y'all kiss my black
and white ass".

But before he could say, they went to some breaking news
about a terrorist planned attack that can not yet be proved.

President Obama is the truth, that most people can't see
he understands that (all) the people of America have got to be free
and educated to compete at the world level
or our future generations will be lost forever.

Hargis
9/9/2011

EVIL...UGLY
RESPONSIBILITY

October was filled with rain, heat, and snow
      from sunny California to Baltimore.
Economy is bad in every state
      marriages are breaking up at an alarming rate.
Everybody is looking, trying to find jobs
      to feed their children, no one wants to starve.

There was a shooting that took place in a Salon (out west)
      an ex-marine was pissed and wearing a bullet proof vest.
84% of all our fish comes from across the way
      but only 2% (the report say) is checked by 'FDA'.

A beautiful black woman, working for 'AFG'
      running a scam with a smile, taking millions you see
because Americans are greedy, always trying to push their luck
      making it easy to get scammed, easy to get fucked.

Another baby is missing...another child raped
      another drive-by shooting...another crime of hate.
Protesters are 'sitting in' in most cities across this land
      trying to make a point about the finances of the rich man.

The politicians are still doing their thang
      pointing at the President for all the blame
where has all the love and unity for each other gone
      or is this the way it has been all along?

It is written that in the last days, 'every eye will see'
      the evil and the ugly that have control over you and me
technology is a tool that sophisticates evil with-in itself
      by moving faster than your sense of time and destroying your health.

God sent President Obama as a warning to us all
       but the Pharaohs of America are trying to cut off his balls
President Obama said lets educate the people and treat them well
       the Pharaohs said...because of you, we'll send them all to hell.

The sea of technology was parted when blacks began to awake
       but the distributors of racism decided to step up their hate
there are some black folks up-holding the evil and the ugly of today
       influenced by the money that the devil is willing to pay.
There are some truth in the bible that even the writers couldn't hide
       about the beast, his actions, and about how he has lied.
There is so much wrong in this world that can't be right
       so much ugly in the streets with their minds uptight.
Everybody has a responsibility of doing something before they die
       if nothing else...step up and ask the question "WHY".

Hargis
12/11/11

"A FEW FACTS"

2012 will be here in a few days...2011 is going out in a blaze
     for those who are keeping score,
there were so much shit this year...everybody should be in fear
     because no one knows what's in the future store.

There were people stolen, raped, and killed...respected people in the community
(their freakishness revealed)
     all caught on tape for everyone to see,
companies and banks are going under...financial troubles (it makes you wonder)
     what happened to all the M O N E Y?

There were shootings, fires, and bombs...sit-ins, riots, and children killed by their moms
     no one is exempted from this hell,
this man you have known all your life...killed his three children and his wife
     too much pressure after his finances failed.

Evil raised its' ugly head...many countries leaders ended up dead
     the CIA found 'big bonuses' under their early X-Mas tree,
thousands have died...because someone lied
     about 'freedom' being the same as 'democracy'.

In every county, in every State...in every city they are preaching hate
     in Kentucky, a church won't let interracial couples in,
where are those who say they believe...in humanity when there is a need
     racism...an old American friend.

On Capital Hill...they were trying to make deals
     one is: to make it harder for blacks to vote,
today many blacks can't see...the real E N EM Y
     and can't feel his hands around their throats.

Out west, in Hollywood...in the streets a man stood
        shooting at every car passing by,
one driver got shot in the neck...trying to see(what did he expect?)
        the reason he was shooting...no one knew why
        but the L.A. police knew he had to die.

America (at this point) is open wide...anything, anywhere can be done inside
        the leadership has accepted the devils' plan,
some call it progress...to others it just a test
        proof...Congress 'refused' yo work hand-in-hand.

Don't be surprised if we become a military state...control by those who
are filled with hate
        their only love is money and power,
they will have us rocking and rolling...dancing and smiling until all of
our finances are stolen
        before we realize that our 'freedom' is in the last hour.

Hargis
12/13/11

2012
A YEAR IN REVIEW

Two thousand and twelve...was a year filled with hell
   civilization dame near went away,
many of the Southern States...openly displayed their hate
   over the communities of Mexicans and 'Gays'.

Politicians went round and round...trying to put each other down
   not caring about the people that put them there,
they wanted the 'White House' back...from this guy (the President)
who was black
   talking about he wants the 'rich' to pay their fare share.

The United States...who many see as great
   was attacked from outside and from within,
our troops are still dying...and the press is still lying
   about who are and who are not our friends.

The Republicans campaign stalled...Nick Romney took a fall
   but that didn't stop their out and out hate,
I don't think they see...that their 'pledge' to disagree
   has started a (political) war in many states.

Texas said from the union they want to SE-cede...because a black
President can't satisfy their needs
   they say that he is responsible for everything that is wrong,
from recalls... to the Congressional section stalls
   and for the weather that has destroyed many homes.

The Pope started texting...about mankind history lessons
   because he feels that the world is turning into 'shit',
earth quakes and storms...brought millions of people some harm
   and the Secretary of States said that "she quit".

The sale of guns are up...to people that don't give a fuck
        they are killing everything that moves,
in the streets, in the movies, and in the malls...in the Spring, Winter,
and Fall
        they are even killing little children in their schools.

The President called forth a committee...to study the gun violets in
every city
        but they didn't really take a stand,
                the mental state America is in...'dogs' and 'guns' are white
                folks best friends
        and their slogan: "when you pry it from my dead hands".

What can be done...about mental ill and guns
        this is what's in everybody head,
so we really don't know why...all those people had to die
        because all the 'shooters' end up dead.

Firemen are called to put out a fire...two or three of them die
        at the hands of another (gun carrying) fool,
people who 'minds' are gone...don't care about right or wrong
        Americans buy guns (a Constitutional rule).

Now everybody is living in fear...at the end of this year
        because death and destruction is everywhere,
and it looks like more is on the way...in January (the 1st day)
        when taxes will be more that most people can bare.

The President and Congress can't agree...about a planned 'budget' and
the fee
        causing most people to suffer more,
the system will automatic make budget cuts...the poor (once again) will
get fucked
        but the 'rich' and their profit will sore.

So here is a little advise...for those who are trying hard to be nice
call your Congressman and curse his 'ass' out,
he has your life and future in his hand...but for you, he won't rake a stand
just let him know that his re-election is in doubt.

Hargis
12/26/12

WHY? WHY? WHY?

In Cali another shooting...in Florida, people are rooting
    because the "Tray Martin" trial is about to begin,
in Boston, a terrorist raised his head...an explosion that left may dead
    in America, it's not news unless it's a sin.

In DC, the 'shit' is still there...the people now know that Congress don't care
    they feel that their representative has left them all alone,
the NSA...is listening to what you say
    in your house and on your cell phones.

In Oklahoma, tornadoes have torn the place up...the Governor shouted
"what the fuck"
    am I and this state going to do,
the people have come to understand...that 'Home Land Security' ain't
the plan
    other cities have put together their own helping crew.

In New York City...life is never pretty
    gangs are snatching cell phones,
in the South, it's a different mind...people are praising Jesus and
committing crimes
    America America an education gone wrong.

The economy they say is looking good...not in my hood
    gangs, drugs, and killings still rule the streets,
technology has taken away life's surprise...because everything is now
computerized
    from job hunting, to dating, to the cooking of your meat.

The dollar use to be back up by gold...but the 'super rich' got that under
control
    now a dollar ain't hardly worth shit,
but 'we the people' work hard all week...it's that pay check we seek
    then turn around and give most of it back to rich.

Business(s) plot day and night...to keep from your mind any 'light'
    that will allow you to keep your cash,
because of our education in 'greed'...and the 'desires' that they feed
    we fall for the scams, the promises, and the ideals that never last.

The younger generations are looking real hard...worrying about their start
    wondering what will be their 'ball of fire',
they are looking at the world in a different light...and see that things just ain't right
    they are asking the question: <u>WHY?</u> <u>WHY?</u> <u>WHY?</u>

Hargus
6/10/2013

150 YEARS
OF PROCESSING

1863 is the year...'Mr. President', "we have blocked all avenues of light to the slaves mind.
You can now go ahead and sign the papers to make them think they are free".

To control our thoughts during and after slavery, we were introduced to nu-imaginable fear.

To control our thoughts after slavery, we were introduced to the 'bible'
    test: the killing of Martin Luther King Jr.
    results: riots, and burnings all over the nation.
    Solution: we were introduced to Capitalism and materialism.

To break up the black family and to destroy any type of unity, we were introduced to birth control, drugs, and self-destruction
    test: Rodney King
    results: riots, burnings, and stealing
    solution: more capitalism, more drugs, TV/movies, and a black President.

To destroy any future leadership within the black community, we were introduced to gang violence (drive-by), imprisonment, death to our youth
    test: Tray Martin
    results; black people (taken into consideration their homes, cars, jobs, friends, and
    images) intellectually reviewed the situation.

"PROCESS COMPLETE"
Mr. President, "we have successfully blocked all avenues of light to our slaves mind
2013...but just in case...we've got Al and Jessie standing by".

Hargis
7/14/2013

MONEY TALKS AND BULLSHIT WALKS

To my dear beloved Brothers and Sister:
America is a Capitalist Society, which mean that:
"Money talks and bullshit walks.

Whenever there is an injustice done to a Black man or a Black woman, we meet, march, and sing. Sometimes we tare up some shit (be it our own shit) but we tare it up. Most of the times, the injustice leads to 'money' because:
"Money talks and bullshit walks.

We would like to think that marriage is based on the 'love of two people'. But when the divorce kicks in, it's all about money...why?
"Money talks and bullshit walks".

What do you think would happen if every black man and black woman stop playing sports in Florida? And if no black entertainer...entertain in Florida? They would take that 'Stand Your Ground Law' and throw it in the ocean...why? Because:
"Money talks and bullshit walks.

Remember Martin Luther King Jr. in Alabama, Black people stop riding the bus. They changed the laws.

Americas' God is money. Whenever there is a tragedy in America (rain, snow, fire, tornadoes, hurricanes, etc), the first thing they want to know is how much has the damage cost.
"Money talks and bullshit walks.

President Obama say "buy America made products", but everyone in America knows that America made products are shit. Shit with a label of 'recall' attached to it.

America, America Oh!!! say can you see
we know that <u>"Money talks and bullshit walks"</u>
from sea to shining sea.

Hargis
7/24/13

I'M JUST SAYING

In every city and every state…
there are crimes of passion and crimes of hate
      too much love will make you mad,
a man and his wife argue a lot…
one morning they were both found shot
      a relationship gone bad.

A mother using the drug 'meth'…
so high, brought about her baby's death
      then threw her body in a trash can,
she let out a sigh and went back and got high…
told the investigators and the world a lie
      that her child was stolen by a black man.

A school teacher was wrong in what she did…
when she fucked one of her kids
      she cried and said it was love(not lust),
her husband couldn't get that in his head…
so he shot her again and again until she was dead
      kept saying something about marriage and trust.

A policeman in the projects implementing his own rules…
welfare and section 8, he thought they were all fools
      until he was found slumped over in his car seat,
in the hood, he was bad…on the force he was just an ass
      he didn't care about the law, he just loved 'dark meat'.

What is it about life…that will turn a man against his wife?
      And make adults mistreat kids all across this land,
all the stories in this poem are true…our actions in life we need to review
      sometimes we have to take a stand.

DON'T MEAN NOTHING…I'M JUST SAYING

Hargis
7/25/13

DECISIONS IN LIFE

What a year this has been...suffering through adversity with a smile
and a grin
    knowing that the quality of life is getting worst,
organizations are falling apart...overweight people with bad hearts
    some people were robbing and killing just to drench their thirst.

Racism and hatred are still in play...sick minds (with power) want to
do things their way
    keeping fear in the air all across this land,
what is kind of sad...is that bulling is getting bad
    no one is teaching children to take a stand.

UN-employment benefits are going away ...making it hard for some to
live from day to day
    crime in the city is already sky high,
if you think yesterday was hard...just wait until tomorrow starts
    those that 'got' will be asking "why".

Lottery is one of Americas' biggest sin...making people think they can win
    so much money, from so many games,
the Government computers control the games and the cash...America
is 'pimping' your fat ass
    you give up all of your money with no shame.

President Obama has a plan...to give health care to every woman and man
    but his haters are saying the plan is no good,
people are dying everyday...because most insurance they can afford to pay
    especially the insurance they are pushing in the hood.

There is still a war in the Middle East...because no one wants to live in peace
    as 'defined' by the enemy they despises,
babies are still been born...in this land that is torn
    at apart from each and every side.

Some say it's that soil...that is rich with 'oil'
    others say it's all about religion,
thousands of lives every day...get taken away
    because the 'devil' won't allow a peaceful decision.

Back in the States...we have to deal with racism and hate
    when they raise their ugly heads,
the President is getting no respect...from people who minds are set
    against anything that he may have said.

This is an election year...the Democrats have their fear
    that the Republicans might get all the votes,
they will have control of the 'Hill'...forcing the President to accept
their deals
    changing 'policies' and destroying the peoples' hope.
"All this shit will blow your mind...by moving faster that your sense
of time"

Hargis
6/19/14

DID YOU KNOW

DID YOU KNOW...
The years 2013 and 2014 were no different from 2012...wars, drive-
by(s), and the President is still catching hell
    distrust and confusion are growing large,
E-Bola is spreading like fire...making hand shakes and hugs just a desire
    and prescription drugs are stopping people hearts.

DID YOU KNOW...
E-bola is in Texas but it won't be long...before it will knock on the door
of your home
    and asking for the lives of you and your kids,
they say that E-Bola was made...like syphilis, birth-control, and aids
    by America scientist who secrets are hid.
They always experiment on blacks...it's a fact
    because we are the children of God,
the war is still a struggle...between the devil and others
    but these problems 'money' won't solve.

DID YOU KNOW...
The police are still killing our youth everyday...the 'so called' leaders
just ask the people to pry
    but it's JUSTICE that the people cry,
most of the killers never get time...the Grand Jury is always justifying
the crime
    the Bloods and the Cribs need to organize and do some 'real'
    drive-by(s).

DID YOU KNOW...
Some people think it is funny...but everything is about money
    and praying don't get you anywhere,
it's been over two thousand years...since Jesus was killed
    how much more in (his name) can the people bare?

DID YOU KNOW...
That Isis is taking over the Middle East...Obama and others are asking them to seize
　　　but all they got was 'cut off heads' and fuck you,
those in the know say...that Isis was created by the 'CIA'
　　　and was given 'US WEAPONS' to help form their crew.

DID YOU KNOW...
The truth is in the air...depend on how much you care
　　　to open up your mind to understand,
our education is sprinkled with truth and tricks...that fill our minds with lots of shit
　　　so that the community in which we live don't have any plans.

Now they can kill, rape, rob us at will...and all we do is pray that we heal
　　　because we've been made to think that our lives aren't worth a thing,
we just try to pay our bills on time...that should be a crime
　　　and stay sleep because we 'love' to dream.

So the question to you...is to 'whom' are you being true
　　　to yourself, your religion, your family, or your State,
they are trying to eliminate blacks..no matter where (it's a fact)
　　　you must never forget that America was and still is rooted in killing and hate.

DID YOU KNOW...
DID YOU REALLY KNOW...
DID YOU?

Hargis
10/22/14

SUBMISSION
TO THINGS WE WHOLD DEAR

What are the things that we fear...are they the things that we hold dear
      like the love of money, property, jobs, and fame,
we give up our dignity and human rights...without a fight
      because we fear the police, politicians, and gangs.

Many of us can't see...that there is no equality
      because TV has made our life one big rage,
most of us think we are grown...but nothing in our community do we own
      so we get shot, beat, robbed, and tazed.

The land-lords...they over charge
      they don't give a shit,
they give us 'EDT' cards and section 8...to keep our minds in a certain state
      having us selling drugs, sex, and children just to get a fix.

Community preachers get us to pray...that's how they get their pay
      having us thinking that they have a personal relationship with God,
but it's the Governments' plan...to eliminate and keep down the
black man
      they don't care if he is shot or starve.

Now our girls have babies with no man around...our sons are justified
in getting shot down
      in every hood in every State,
there are a few that do escape...this 'death' pool of hate
      some come back to show others how to unlock the gate.

The schools and education in the hood...is not very good
      the drop out rate is very high,
the streets get their minds...quick money, but lots of time
      killing each other while our families cry, asking why?

So what are the things that we fear...and the things that we hold dear?
    Are they one in the same?
For those who submit to the plan...will never understand
    and will never know who is really the blame.

Hargus
11/13/14

"WAR"
THE STRUGGLE CONTINUES

Shot down in the streets with his hands in the air…
people standing around did nothing but stare.

They were choking him he couldn't breath, he said it many times…
it was all on film, but the Grand jury said 'no crime'.

He was just a kid…look at what the police did…
shot him dead, because of what someone said.

The judiciary system is no joke it's allowing others to kill black folks
but all across this land…there are people starting to take a stand
for what the police and others are doing to the black man.

Now they got this 'punk' name Charles…who has lost the love of himself
he talks on the tube, not knowing that he is being used
thinking he is cool, because he has a little wealth.
He is saying things that are not right…but he has to protect white or
go home to a fight.

When you look back over our past…here in America (over five hundred
it has last)
mistreatment, violent, and death are what we have had,
our families they broke up…they didn't give a fuck
now we pray and beg them for justice (ain't that sad?).

In recent years…a lot of mothers have cried those tears
when their sons were shot down UN-just,
but nothing gets done…just like when we use to get hung
now the killers are asking for forgiveness and trust.

Is it just me...or are all the cities hiring the same type of police
the ones with the mentally of the 'klan',
most of them got the same profile...red neck, racist, and wild.

We talk, talk, talk...and we pray and walk
but most of the killers are set free,
they have finally showed their hand...the DA and the jury they call 'Grand'
America has openly declared war on the black man.

Hargis
12/13/14

BUSH AND CHANEY
"TORTURE"

I was watching the news the other day...listening to Dick Chaney discussing
Guantanamo Bay
    and the torture of lives that was performed,
it was about the technique of pain...designed to fuck with your brain
    trying to keep others from doing the "USA" any harm.

He said everything they did was approved...and they played by the rules
    the goal was to get the information they needed,
Dick said the CIA report wasn't true...and the techniques wasn't new
    but the enemy's mentaity had to be treated.

He said the program was good...but what had to be understood
    that the '911' attack was an act of war,
some people felt that they were deceived...but there are 3,000 Americans
who can no longer breath
    and families are depraved of their joy.

This show was called 'meet the press'...and they had other guests
    that gave their points of view,
they talked about Dick and the boys...the CIA and some of their toys
    and some of the things that the American people never knew.

All of this got started during Jr. Bush time...the master of international crimes
    the President who had his own 'hit list',
today, he struts around proud...when talking about torture (he smiles)
    eight years at the helm, put us all at risk.

Chaney and Bush did what they had to do...to protect me and you
    and to honor those that died,
that was one of Americas' worst of times...Guantanamo Bay (to me) was fine
    I thought about all the families (I cried).

Hargis
12/15/14

AMERICA DO YOU SEE WHAT I SEE?

I was born in the hood...but it has to be understood
      that many times I have been knocked to my knees
I'm in my right mind...at least most of the time
      but what I see us what I see.

"America do you see what I see"?

I see fear in the eyes of those who walk the streets
I hear fear in the voice of those who are trying to teach.
I see children who are afraid of walking to the store
I see some fathers turning their wife(s) and daughters into whores.
I see families and communities being torn apart
I see Government issued 'drugs' that are stopping people hearts.
I see educational systems that are falling into ruins
I see no 'love' for one another, because everyone is suing.

"America do you see what I see"?

I see the homeless community growing bigger everyday
some got 'degrees' but no jobs and no place to stay.
I see corruption in the Government on all life levels
I see some (so called) leaders, preachers, and teachers being exposed as devils.
I see some Congressmen stimulating racism all across this land
targeting the President just because he's a black man.
I see police killing people at the blink of an eye
I see 'no' justice for families, everyone is wondering Why?
I see the end product of years of deceit, destruction, and death
I see where chemical induced foods are destroying the people health.
I see where many babies are dying at birth
because in the lives of some mothers...drugs come first.
I see that in America...money is God
so in the name of Jesus...people deceive, kill, and rob.

"America do you see what I see"?
"America do you see"?
<u>What I see</u>

Hargis
1/9/15

"A REMINDER"

For too many years...we have had to shed tears
    in this land that everyone say is great,
some of the children to whom we give birth...have been placed back
into the earth
    by those who we trust and the spreaders of hate.

Our history is our history...and there is no mystery
    we have experienced nothing but pain since we met the white man
many of us have tried hard to forget...all of the ugliness
    that we have suffered all across this land.

What we need to understand...that our suffering is the history of this man
    and he keeps 'his' children historically informed,
kill the Red, Black, and the Brown...that's how we got down
    my reward to you will be: 'no harm'.

They show how they took this land...from the Red man
    and enslaved you and me,
they want the ugly to grow...remember the Alamo?
    And every year they re-product these movies so their children can see.

We have tried to integrate...into this hellish world of hate
    and still they value the life of a dog over us,
they think our lives ain't worth shit...because in their world we don't fit
    but when we are killed, we just cry, march, sing, and fuss.

Now I'm not advocating anything...but what is the 'America Dream'?
    For us, it's something of a mystery,
we speak their language and dance to their beat...and some got money
and some love white meat
    and some are trying very hard to forget our "History"

Hargis
5/15/15

"SIDE AFFECTS"

Prescription drugs have got everybody hooked…
Pharmacies are the suppliers and the doctors are keeping the books.
They got a pill for your ass…if you got insurance…or some cash.

If you got a cold and a running nose…listen to what you are been told:
    take this pill one time a day…but three times you need to pray
    it will make you bleed so you can't sneeze, give you dry mouth, a hard on,
    but you can't shit
    it will make feel like you want to die, but you have no tears to cry…
    and in pain, you are understanding this.
    But if your throat swells up …and people look at you and say 'oh fuck'
    see your doctor right away
    it's been clinically proven to kill 'only' one out ten…so feel safe my friend
    because it has been approved by the FDA.

If you are obesity or just fat…there is pill for that.
If your head hurts and you are going blind…and having problems with your heart or spin
there is a pill that will set you free
but if your stomach hurt…and your dick don't work
your doctor is the person to see.
    He's got a prescription that will make you wild.
    He's got a prescription that will make you smile.
    He's got a prescription that will ease your pain.
    He's got a prescription that will keep you sane.
Prescription drugs have been approved in every State.
They got stuff that will put you to sleep and keep you awake.
They have legalized marijuana for those that are having problems seeing.
They came up with an adult dipper for those who are having problems peeing.

Side affects can be deadly if you are not aware…
the pharmacy and the doctors, they really don't care
because making money is their goal.. and prescription drugs are worth
more than gold.
Every time you visit your doctor, he gives you a scrip for a new pill
remember he us not trying to cure anything…that's not part of the deal.
If you are not coughing up blood, just stay away
your doctor is not God, how long you live…he has nothing to say.
Also, remember, that with prescription drugs…the doctor will become rich
but for you and me…the side affect is a 'bitch'.

Hargis
5/30/15

SAME OLD SHIT

The last week of October, around Halloween
confusion, discontent, and more bull shit than you have ever seen.

Every morning you wake up and find that someone has been shot
people are begging for mercy, asking that the killing stop.

The police is on automatic, killing blacks time after time
not worrying about jail because they don't think it's a crime.

Gangs are terrorizing the hood but won't fuck with the police
a few drive-by(s)...some of the police killings will cease.

When a killing take place in the hood all the community do is pray
The so-called leaders don't have a plan so they ask the people to lay.

The gangs do a lot of killing they don't care about the grave or jail
it's the honor they seek sending another to hell.

The Chinese are mad over a phone call
the Mexican are still saying are not paying for a wall.

People are protesting all over the earth
because the USA has UN-leased the 'devil' by giving him birth.

A Presidential is in demand
millions of people are taking a stand.

Which direction will America take?
progress, destruction, love or hate?

And what about 'war' will it come again?
Or will we bond and make strong friends?

Hargis
5/10/16

"I'VE SEEN"

In America I have traveled from state to state...I have been shown a lot of love and I've seen a lot of hate
    I've also seen the beauty of this land,
I've seen moments that were crucial...and people uniting for solutions
    that's the real intellect of man.

I've seen trees up rooted and bldg fold...I've seen weather so bad that cars and planes couldn't roll
    and people homes floating down the street,
I've been in churches, Mosques, and Temples a like...I've seen leaders of religion take away the people rights
    I've seen some of those people bounce back from defeat.

I've seen babies born with drugs in their vain...cause their pregnant mothers was getting high and with no shame
    thinking that no one 'really' care,
I've seen people marching, singing, and crying the blues...but it's the Government grants money that makes the rules
    and those that don't understand, keep saying 'unfair'

I've seen people get mistreated because they are poor...I've seen the power of money turn women into whores
    because money is the God of this land,
I've seen families uprooted...and business looted
    because of money and the evil of man

I've not trying to be mean...but I've seen what I've seen
    and money is in control of all thoughts,
you can say what you will...but truth can get you killed
    but seeing what I've seen is what this poem is all about.

Hargis
8-16-16

'DONALD (THE DEVIL) TRUMP'

Most people say...if you vote things will go your way
      not in my hood,
every four years...they address our fears
      but nothing is really understood.

Evil is in charge...and living large
      I'm talking about Hillary and Donald the same,
a vote is a vote...it give some people hope
      you would think that (by now) we should know the game.

But here we are...cheering for our political star
      who wants to move to Capital Hill,
and unleash their plan...to destroy every man
      by taking away his sprite and his free will.

Donald don't know what to do….and Hillary ain't been true
      but their followers don't give a fuck,
Evil is in control...and will take your soul
      while you sitting around wishing them 'good luck'.

If Donald gets in...he will bring out all of your sins
      and bring about a racial conflict,
everyone will be confused...like his non-credited school
      everything we do will be at risk.

Donald's evil is pure...he is the devil and that's for sure
      nothing he says make sense,
what will the people do...with Donald and his crew?
      Cause every situation will be tense.

If you are reading or listening to this poem...don't be alarm
      because GOD takes care of all things,
but he has to let you see...what's inside of you and me
      and will allow you to wonder, pray, and dream.

"The people must be free"

Hargis
8-9-16

WE WILL SEE

THE 2016 Presidential race...is been done in bad taste
      because Donald has taken the low road,
in each and every State...Donald is preaching fear and hate
      but in reality, he is stealing souls.

I can see the head lines in my head...Donald announced that freedom is dead
      and that Democracy will soon be gone,
speaking from his place of rest...he blamed it on Congress and the press
      and them niggas who keep marching and singing them dame songs.

The American dream has fallen into a hole...people are in debt can't
find that pot of gold
      following Donald Trump,
with Hillary, it wouldn't be the same...she understands the importance
of the game
      and know that sometimes you have to shake that rump.

They are talking about women who have been raped...and police that
have escaped
      the just hand of the law,
they are talking about deporting them all and building a wall
      their debates and actions are raw.

We will see...if history
      will come into play this year,
or will evil take control...and steal every mind and soul
      and leave Americans with confusion and fear.
The people must be free

Hargis
10-13-16

"COMING TOGETHER"

I was at this rally...in southern Caly
  when it began to rain pretty hard,
everybody stood still...as if it was against their will
  that's when I felt a pain in my heart.

This tall black man...was talking about taking a stand
  against Grand Juries that let killers go,
I over came the pain...and the cold rain
  as my knowledge began to grow.

The speaker was cool...and talked real smooth
  pointing out fact after fact after fact,
He said these juries were police friend...ex-police and their kin
  and against the victims the cards are stacked.

A woman stood up and screamed...and said that she used to be a part
of that team
  until they beat her husband (they say by mistake),
he was an undercover cop...ID(eed) himself but they didn't stop
  this beating was done out of pure hate.

All charges were dropped...because they were white cops
  the Grand Jury justified their case,
what made me so mad...after they beat him pretty bad
  they tried to tell us that it had nothing to do with race.

Another speaker took the mike...and said we have to learn to fight
  the system and all its' mysteries,
things haven't changed...4 hundred years we've been mistreated,
murdered, and hanged
  We can start by knowing true history.

Some of you my think you understand...but this is a devilish land
        from sea to shining sea,
Police took the 'red' pill...killing blacks at will
        don't want young blacks thinking they are free.

Blacks are shot down in the streets...hands up or on their knees
        they know that all blacks do is march and cry,
they plot day and night...to direct blacks sight
        they are masters in making the truth seems like a lie.

Many others stood on the stage...expressing their outrage
        about this and about that,
it was getting kind of dark...so we had to depart
        when it was announced the killing of another black.

People march and pray...and always say
        that 'black lives matter'
but when they hear that sound...and see another black man hit the ground
        it seems like 'only' death can bring blacks together.

Hargis
8/18/16

D.T. OR T.D.
DONALD TRUMP OR THE DEVIL

2016 oh what a time...out of the darkness of evil came the master of crime
I'm not talking about robbing banks or selling drugs...killings in the
streets or senior citizen mugs.

It's election year...(a different fear)
  and the politicians are on the move,
the Mafia stay low...because they know
   that politicians are monsters from another school.

The head man himself...who claims he has all the wealth
  is as evil as they get,
he spreads lies all across this land...and channel any man
   because outside of himself, he doesn't give a shit.

Trump won the election even though Hillary got more votes
but this years' run for the 'house' was surely no joke.

Trump and Hillary are both evil but Trump is the all time master
they say he got kicked out of Heaven for calling God a baster.

So now America is set with Trump at the wheel
this time next year there will be no such thing as 'free will'.

D.T. or T.D. they both are the same
but whatever he does, it's someone else who be blamed.

Hargis
11-16-16

'PRESIDENT TRUMP'

Trump won the election and the whole world was shocked...
Hillary got more votes but that don't mean a lot
    It's a crazy world we live in,
People everywhere are protesting the vote...the 'devil' is in the White house, there isn't much hope
    America has just unleashed the master of sin.

He promised to UN-do good and redirect wrong...he informed the people of color to practice new marching songs
    because the real shit is about to go down,
So if you are for Trump or if you think he sucks...he doesn't give a fuck
    cause he is really not for any skin color that's black or brown.

He got all the power in the palm of his hands...his foreign policy is: I am the man
    so who knows what he is going to do,
He has talked about street violent and building walls...bringing jobs back and 'trump' malls
    He wants to make America White Again for him and his crew.

Black people of America, it's time to annie up the pot...because life in our communities is about to get hot
    when Trump reverse the Orders that Obuma signed,
a lot of people can't see...that the evil in this man won't let you be
    his objective is to glorify evil and crime.

"The people must be free"

Hargis
11-16-16

"2016 SLAVERY"

Black men are still getting shot...by racist cops
    and no charges are been filed,
this policeman said he was scead...but shot an unarmed black man 5
times in his head
    it was caught on camera in front of a crowd.

Let a policeman get shot...the whole city will be on lock
    down for as long as it take,
then they want us to know...that he was a 'hero'
    but in my hood he Represents hate.

Whites have always killed black...that's a historical fact
    and they never saw it as a crime,
I know that it sounds insane...but ain't nothing changed
    through out the history of time.

Now here we are today...still on our knees trying to pray
    asking God to forgive those who are doing us wrong,
we are what they made...fancy dressed slaves
    existing in the 21st century zone.

We cry and we moan...cuss and march until we get home
    to watched ourselves on TV,
we don't shoot or kill...we are just trying to live
    in a society (thinking) that we are free.

Hargis
11-30-16

69

HE WAS CALLED

Trump is making decisions...that's costing people millions
     in profits, jobs, and stocks,
he's got 43 days...before his White House parade
     then the cork from the champagne can be popped.

He was on the cover of time...blew some people minds
     he was named 'the man of the year',
this society in which we live...make you wake you want to kill
     out of your ignorance and fear.

The White house used to be Black...the red necks had a neverous attack
     working hard to up root his every move,
when they failed...they placed a call to the boss of hell
     asking for a leader who can rule.

Trump came on the scene...disrespectful and mean
     turning everything upside down,
he said and did some shit...that made most people sick
     but he was White house bound.

Shaking things up is his goal...out with the new bring back the old
     is his promise to the red necks,
just don't forget who he is...the devil who will lie, cheat, and steal
     the most evil person you ever met.

The people must be free

Hargis
12-7-16

"IT'S ABOUT THAT TIME"

Trump thee elect...got people in the hood taking bets
    that he won't last the whole four years,
he goes after anyone who disagree...trying to make the whole world see
    that he has no fears.

Before he gets sworn in...he's making enemies and friends
    by trying to change US polices as he goes,
right or wrong...weak or strong
    people are just praying that America doesn't fold.

The attitude of whites have change...as if Trump has recharged their brain
    racist actions are on the rise,
UN-presidential is what they say...when Trump does things his way
    but everyone know that he speaks mostly lies.

He is turning over his business to his folks...everyone know that it's a joke
    now people are talking about an interest conflict,
but Trump is Trump...and he'll tell you to kiss his rump
    cause the whole world know that he doesn't give a shit.

He is tweeting and talking on the TV everyday...cause he wants America
to know what he's got to say
    but he will change his meaning every now and then,
he is not wrapped very tight...and his 'great' means 'white'
    a few more days and it will all begin.

Legally I mean...a racist dream
    because they removed a black man from the hill
those who are wise...will not be surprise
    if Trump was shot or killed.

Don't get me wrong...I'm not singing that song
    but in America everything goes,
and it's an actual fact...that anyone can get whacked
    from babies to Presidents to hoes.

THE PEOPLE MUST BE FREE

Hargis
12-29-16

EVIL IN THE HOUSE

The devil is in...and he is raising the level of sin
　　from the White House in DC,
even some who gave him their votes...are calling him a Presidential joke
　　they are wondering now, how long will we be free.

Two months have gone by...and Trump is still saying "I"
　　there is dis-content all over this land,
he promised a lot through out his campaign...and many thought he
was insane
　　but deceit and confusion are the weapons of this evil man.

His cabinet is filled with the rich...who don't give a shit
　　about the problems of the poor,
if America was for sell...Trump will make a deal with hell
　　if it results in him owning another store.

Now there is this 'wall'...that got Trump by the balls
　　he is saying that the Mexicans will pay for it,
but Mexico said "fuck you...and your crew"
　　because "we ain't paying for shit".

Trump just ignores what they say...but insures the American people
they will pay
　　but first, we have to come out of our pockets to build,
he blame it all on the press...Hillary, and his wife's blue dress
　　because in his mind, he is the only one that's for real.

If anyone challenge his words...they hit his real mean nerve
　　Trump try to publicly dis-credit them for life,
he is trying to undo what Obama has done...not knowing the millions
that will be harmed,
　　but he is working hard trying to make America 'White'. (again)

Hargis
3/1/17

1ST QUARTER REPORT

The President is in the hole...in need of new willing souls
     to get to the next level,
they are checking him in and out...saying fuck his clout
     they don't understand that Trump is the devil.

He is using his son and daughter...can't trust any other
     to give him good advise,
but everywhere he turns...he is getting burned
     now his voters are began to think twice.

The investigators are on his ass...about Russia and the relationship his people had
     before and during the election,
Trump is saying that the Democrats are the blame...trying to redirect the game
     and to get that political 'erection'.

Trump tell lies and this everybody know...that's why his Presidential rating is so low
     but he is telling the people that everything is going great,
none of his decisions can be reached...people are now talking about impeach
     he is blaming that on the news reporters and their hate.

Trump 1st 100 days aren't looking to good...but one thing has to be understood
     that Trump is the devil in a human form,
he was called...to inflate the ball
     and he doesn't give a shit about who he harms.

Hargis
3/3/17

"CDF"
CONFUSION DECEIT FEAR

2017...nightmare or dream?
    Depending on who you are,
Politicians and Preachers are still lying...parents are still crying
    about the shooting deaths that have gone too far.

Three months into the year...everyone has some fear
    of the streets and / or the dark,
war in Europe and the middle east...is never going to seize
    because Isis is fighting from their heart.

What's new is now old...the weak is now bold
    because shit today just don't make sense,
the President is tweeting lies...some of his cabinet are sleeping with spies
    and the black man is still getting lynched.

The safety and sanity of life is gone...nothing is based on right or wrong
    they had to pass 'sex laws' in this land,
homosexuals had their solution...but it took a revolution
    now man can legally marry another man.

In America life is a bitch...if you ain't rich
    having a lot of money will make you think that you are a god,
it will improve your schemes...and help develop your dreams
    it will, also, allow you to kill and rob.

If you are Red, Black, or Brown...this system is designed to keep you down
    and have you thinking 'that's just the way life is',
true selves are now been seen...those you thought were good are now
been mean
    showing what they have been thinking for years.

Don't get me wrong...this is not another 'sad song'
  there are 'some things' that are been done,
don't need no tears...these actions are for real
  but we have to get together and save our young.

Hargis
3/16/17

WHO GOT THE POWER?

The Republicans are on the move...they think that they got their groove
     to repeal Obama Care,
they are obsessed with this man...and will do what ever they can
     to erase his name from the Presidential air.

Trump is a man who makes deals...that will get a lot of people killed
     a Politician he is not,
Trump thinks he is doing well...but he is taking America right to hell
     his lies and deceits, he can't stop.

He threaten Americans about the money for his wall...
if he doesn't get it, he will let America fall
     "shut it down" are the words he used,
but after checking out his mind...and the reality of time
     the wall situation, he removed.

Now he is making his tax reform sound sweeter than honey...
this is to ensure that the rich will get to keep their money
     and the poor will have more money to spend,
his reform is a bunch of shit...because the poor will have to spend all
they get
     for the economy to mend.

Times in America are tight...what was done in the dark is coming to light
     if you believe in the 'so called' good book,
America has become evil as hell...Trump is the warrant of this jail
     and the 'power' is in the hands of the crooks.

Hargis
4/24/17

AMERICA, AMERICA

America America: do you hear what I hear…
    the masses of your people are living in fear
    of gangs, racism, and Government too,
    afraid to get stopped…by a crooked cop
    or dragged off a plane by the airport crew.

America America: can you hear the people cry…
    life is getting worst and they want to know why
    and why you think drugs are the answer to all things,
    from birth to death…you have fucked with their health
    keeping them sleep and thinking about dreams.

America America: the people are trying to understand…
    how did the 'ugly mentality' get control of this land
    and set up shop in every State,
    stealing their wills…through crooked deals
    and intensifying their abilities to hate.

America America: you were once 'the land of the free'…
    understood and loved from sea to shinning sea
    before 'profit' raised her head,
    now people are bold…and out of control
    and for that money they will shoot you dead.

America America: what are you going to do…
    to ensure that your future will be true
    because the whole world is watching you.

Hargis
4/28/17

DEAR POLITICIANS

To the Republicans and Democrats you are both the same...
getting rich off the people playing that good guy//bad guy game
    someday it will come to a head,
you were elected by the people to represent their thoughts...
once you reached Capital Hill you forgot what it was all about
    you have to be mindful who is sleeping in your bed.

You were young, eager and filled with fire...
but that 'money' on the Hill made you change your desire
    and taught you another language too,
now you are working for 'the big bucks'...and your district you don't
give a fuck
    now you think that they are working for you.

When a good bill is on the floor...'big bucks' tell you to abstain and
walk out the door
    but you know it's not right,
at first it stayed in your mind...but you gave in with in a matter of time
    deceiving the people doesn't happen over night.

So been a Democrat or a Republican is not it...America needs unity
and an up to date fix
    to compete in the world today,
she used to be first...because she had that thirst
    but you and money have put her in a whorish way.

Hargis
4/28/17

ALL AROUND THE WORLD

It's almost May...and in the news today
      is terrorism and the threats of war,
there is still killings in the streets...and safety (many still seek)
      inside and out a far.

The wall issue is going around and around...most people are concerned
with the Government 'shutting down'.
      And what will come out of Trumps mouth,
he is making very little progress...his people have to confess
      and nothing is making it to the House.

Korea is doing their thing...China and Japan are trying to hang
      while Europe is constantly under attack,
in America, most of the states...are displaying racial and religion hate
      and there is an increase in the drug called crack.

Trump is on the air...still talking about Obama Care
      the wall and tax reform,
his first one hundred days were wild...he acted like an old ass child
      not caring about the people he harmed.

He dropped bombs in the Middle East...trying to get Syria to cease
      the use of 'nerve gas'
Trump and his party have just about split...because he talk so much shit
      now the people is wondering how long is he going to last.

Hargis
4/24/17

DARK DAYS

I thought I heard it all...when Trump talked about 'the wall'
    but the problems in the house is insane,
the investigators are in their shit...some aids got fired and some them quit
    others are pointing at others to blame.

The FBI head...is lucky he ain't dead
    with all the shit he has done,
they said that Comey did wrong...so Trump told him to move on
    after praising him like he was his son.

Now all of his Mope head are talking like we can't remember...lying
that Trump has been trying to remove him since November.
    But loved him when he talked about Hillary 'e-mails'
    when he wouldn't drop the Russian prob...Trump tried hard to
    steal his soul
    now he wants him to be put in jail.

Most of the Republicans are trying to roll with the punch...trying hard
to protect Trump
    for it is written and the writing is on the wall,
there is no escape...the house in in bad shape
    and Trump may have to take the fall.

We all remember 'Tricky Dick' and what he did...but that will look like
child play, when they blow this lid
    if the truth be told,
Trump heart is dark...in fact it is charred
    you know like the 'black hole'

Hargis
5/11/17

THE STATE OF THE HOUSE

The question has to be asked...is it a lie or is it a fact
    that America is in a state of shock?
Between Trump lies...and the Russian spies
    the people are taking in a lot.

The CIA, the FBI, and the Secret Service too...Comey, Flynn, and the
rest of Trump crew
    all are trying to save their ass,
Trump is constantly tweeting...about how he is been mistreated
    his Presidency may not last.

Comey is set to testify...Trump is already calling him a lie
    and is threatening him with some unknown tapes,
in an earlier poem, I said...I'm surprised that Comey ain't dead
    cause the President Office could be at stake.

Trump asked for his loyalty and he said no...so Trump told him he had to go
    his honesty is not what Trump needs,
he wants to be in control...of your will and your soul
    Trump is a good example of the real 'American Greed'.

He has threaten everyone he knows...that doesn't go alone with his show
    most of them think that he is good,
but America is falling like bricks...thanks to Trump and his shit
    and you know what we think of him in the hood.

His Education Director tried to make a speech...they 'boo' her so hard
she had to retreat
    his choice has the educational world upset,
young people understand...they ain't like their 'old' man
    they aren't waiting for the ugly affect.

Some Democrats are throwing out hints...talking about impeachment
    if he doesn't straighten up his act,
some of the Republicans are not far behind...saying that Trump needs
to fall in line
    or his head is gona roll, and that's a fact.

Hargis
5/15/17

THE TRIP

Trump is over seas...kissing ass, trying to please
    seeking help from other lands,
with so much pressure on his back...and Presidential experience he
total lacks
    but he is finally asking for a helping hand.

His 'mope heads' sort let it slip...saying Trump is on an organizing trip
    to tell other countries what they should be doing,
we know that he doesn't know the ropes...giving others false hopes
    and directions that can only lead to ruins.

Trump is on a mission to kill...the mind and thoughts of free will
    and dark people is his goal,
he is visiting Muslims, Buddhist, and Hindu a like...the people he
wouldn't let on America flights
    no one knows how this trip will unfold.

Some of his followers are beginning to see the light...saying that Trump
is making life tight
    while he is in the learning stage,
some still think he is great...but that's really up for debate
    because 65% of the country thinks he is an out rage.

The magic number (days) is nine...we hope that he doesn't committee
any crimes
    by saying shit he ain't suppose to,
but you can never tell...because his mind is filled with hell
    just remember that everything to him is new.

Hargis
5/22/17

HELP IS ON THE WAY

Another black man died...and justice (once again) was denied
    to his family and friends,
his hands were in the air...but she didn't care
    she just doesn't like black men.

She shot him in the back...and just like that
    his life was taken away,
she sound sincere...but she had some fear
    of not making it home that day.

She had the only gun...he had none
    she said she feared for her life,
it was all caught on tape...and the jury did deliberate
    not guilty...'oh shit'...shouted his wife.

Will this bullshit ever end...the killing of black men
    and will black men ever rise up???
help is on the way...white folks better learn how to pray
    because this generation ain't gona give a fuck.

Hargis
5/22/17

AGAIN AND AGAIN

Trump is at it again...deceiving his friends
      he fired one of his top aids,
he praised the man in the past…but the man wouldn't kiss his ass
      he said his confident in him has fade.

To mislead, confuse, and deceive is Trump style...even his most loyal
supporters are saying that Trump is wild
      the first five months of the year,
some of the things he wants have been put into play...people all over the
world are coming together to pray
      because Trump has got the power they fear.

Don't forget that Trump was called...and the order was tall
      the Black man has go to go,
Trump is trying his best...to stir up some mess
      then sit back and watch it grow.

So keep your faith in the lord…because the real shit is getting ready to start
      there will be no commercials at all,
it may look crazy...because your mind has gotten lazy
      but how can you get up if you don't believe in the fall.

The things I say are for real...you can laugh, frown, or bring about tears
      but your life is on the line,
poor people are getting fucked...because they don't have the big bucks
      this thing is moving faster than your since of time.

You are being lied to about where to go and who to see...who you are
and who you should be
      if you want to be 'great again',
don't get it wrong...the devil 'IS' on the throng
      in the form of a human being.

Hargis
5/31/17

"EXPOSURE"

Trump is doing it again...telling lies and inspiring sins
    I think it's war he is trying to wage,
Russia, China, and Japan...are saying that something is wrong with this man
    his mouth is sort of setting the stage.

Obama Care he doesn't get...cause his mind is full of shit
    a Politician he is not,
Trump is looking to make a deal...even if it means millions getting killed
    he is cold hearty and think he is as slick as a fox.

Every time he speaks...he makes America seem weak
    because he knows not what he do,
the bible talks about this man...he got 666 in his fore head and his hand
    evil is in his heart and he's after me & you.

Now don't get me wrong...and miss-quote this song.
    Just look at what the man do and say,
he tweets what's on his mind...which should be a crime
    now we have to put our heads between our legs and 'pray'.

America what have we done...put a man in the House who brings about harm
    now many are saying he is a disgrace,
there are some who don't know who he is...so whatever he does they get a thrill
    especial when he talks about 'Gender, religion, and race'.

Trump (and his mentality)has to be...so the world can see
    prophecies have to be for filled,
this war is about creation...not immigration
    and the control of mans free will.

Trump is blowing smoke up our ass...and moving pretty fast
  because he knows that time is running out,
so he is bringing about more confusion that will create delusions
  then introduce himself, so there won't be any doubts.

Hargis
6/30/17

THE MAKING OF WAR

Dear American people...look like we've got the 'grim weeper'
  as the President of the United States,
he has the mentality of a stick...that keep stirring up shit
  the sad part about is he think he is great.

He told the military to load and lock it...his reality he keeps in his pocket
  cause he talks like he wants a war,
there were millions that was backing him up...now most of them are
saying 'what's the fuck'
  this red neck has gone too far.

The klan and the skin heads have gotten bold...marching thru the State
like the days of old
  but they were met with people against their cause,
The President won't say anything...cause the klan and the skin heads
are a part of his team
  now his own party is saying that he has no 'balls'.

This has been going on all year...bullshit from Trump that bringing
about fear
  while the whole world is waiting to see,
oh, he is talking tough...but Korea is calling his bluff
  China and Russia (with Trump) don't agree.

Trump thinks he can do as he choose...but he need to be removed
  before the whole world starts to fight,
he can't get anything done...so he is putting everyone in harm
  he just do not have any in-sight.

Everything Trump has done have failed...if he wasn't rich, his ass would be in jail

money, money, money, money,

poor red neck mothers are looking at him with bright eyes...but soon they'll be in for a surprise

when he says "I need your kids for war, honey".

Hargis
8-13-17

HE'S GOT TO GO

Trump is still opening his mouth...saying things he know nothing about
    thinking he is the 'greatest' President ever,
what is really amazing...that a lot of people don't think he's crazy
    because they know that Trump is the devil.

Trump has gotten comfortable in his skin...thinking that he can always win
    so he text and say what ever is on his mind,
disrespect and confusion...are the tactics the devil uses
    'his' deceptions will become a reality in time.

To keep you confused...he create the news
    to keep your mind off his wrong,
you know that evil don't give a shit...about putting your life at risk
    but cry about the safety of your home.

Trump is the 'devil' in human form...this is my attempt to warn
    you that his worst is on the way,
you may ask, 'how do I know'...because history has shown this show
    now all man can is pray.

He spoke at the UN...and a few said 'a men'
    but most said they were shocked,
about the language he used...sounding like a fool
    and that he should have been stopped.

Then he went down South...still running his mouth
    creating a problem all across this land,
people need to become aware...and realize that he doesn't care
    because Trump is an evil man.

We have had floods and destruction in many States...but he is constantly saying how the Government is doing great
people are dying everyday,
they raised millions in Texas to help those in need...they did the same thing in Florida and everyone was pleased
but the help in Puerto Rico was some how delayed.

There are fires in Calif. And bad weather in the mid-west...Korea is constantly putting their missals to a test
Trump is trying to start a war
NFL is protesting some of the things that Trump has said...but evil is not evil unless it can get into your head
and Trump is really working so far.

There will come a time when everyone will see...get together with each other and agree
that he can't be the USA boss,
between Russia and his tweets...and all of his Congressional defeats
America future is at a loss.

Hargis
9/24/17

DARKNESS ACROSS THE LAND

November 2017...so much violent it makes you want to scream
    is it gun control or mental ill?,
concerts, schools, and churches too...with automated weapons (old and new)
    getting shot talking, walking, or just seating still.

Beauty in America has been taken away...death & destruction is where
ever you stay
    people have become fearful of doing anything,
for many years...Americans have been shedding tears
    because guns are in the hands of those who are mean and can't
    be seen.

Laws are not been enforced...it all about 'that money' of course
    because in America you have got to get paid,
children, women, and men...shooters have no friends
    modern day crime is 'American made'.

The President said he didn't want to talk about controlling guns...it will
take away from the Republican funds
    NRA has got Republicans and red neck under control,
when you look at the history of this land...having a gun is what made
you a man
    and the constitution will bear witness to your soul.

I can't help from thinking out loud...about a person shooting into a crowd
    what kind of pressure was he under,
he was born like all others...through a father and a mother
    but educated with fire and thunder.

Those who are close don't shed any tears...they have been knowing
about his 'state of mind' for years
    they say it was just a matter of time,
but for the many that lye in graves...some could have been saved
    and the communities would have been spared some crying.

If you say something long enough, people will begin to think you are
right... putting them in charge of your mind and your sight
        then justification is sat into play,
but the shooters are out there...armed to the teeth and don't really care
        to them, shooting and killing is the American way.
"may the peace and blessings of God forever be upon us"

Hargis
11/8/17

THE TAKE OVER

Statistics states...that the use drugs is high in every State
        controlled mostly by the Government,
the pharmacies are the cookers...and the Dr. are the pushers
        together they are miking a mint.

I'm talking about drugs in the stores or in the streets...from insurance
agents or dealers you may meet,
        they all have the same affect,
you can get them in the stores, play grounds, or school halls...with cash
money or by pulling down your draws
        it's all about business and the mind set.

To keep you in need...they legalized weed
        in most States, it is allowed to grow,
sit back and think...remember when it used to bad to drink
        and tobacco was a no no.

we moved pass that real fast...after the Government peeped that cash
        they made the street pushers go preach,
now they are in control...of your money and your soul
        and they set up drug goals for you to reach.

Insurance companies let you get drugs free...cause they know that eventually
        you will become hooked,
drug use in America is wild...used by every man, woman, and child
        giving them all that certain look.

"FREE YOUR MIND AND ASS WILL FOLLOW"

Hargis
11/17/17

BYE BYE 2017

17 is gone and 18 is here...and most of Congress are dressed in fear
    because 'the devil' is in charge of the House,
he says things that's not good...and don't care if it's misunderstood
    because his speakers are to keep the public in doubt.

To say that the President is a lair is putting it kind of mild...
but the red-necks of America love his style
    in trying to make America White,
yes he has shaken up DC...but what he has failed to see
    is that the majority of the people are ready to fight.

In 17...Trump was like a dope finn
    getting high off his own lie
Congress is afraid to admit...that he is saying the wrong shit
    they just back away or say bye bye.

His first year in office was the worst in history...to most American
people there is no mystery
    the man is evil thru and thru,
he lied about the wall..and who will pay to have it installed
    now he wants the money from me and you.

Trump shut down the Government...because of this fence
    trying to prove his word is bond,
but we all know the facts...that he doesn't like the Brown and the Blacks
    for a good deal, Trump will sell his own son.

He helped pass a tax reform...that will cause more harm
    unless you are a member of his 'rich crew',
and everybody on the Hill is rich...now ain't that a bitch
    so it will end up being a burden for me and you.

He gave his first speech to the State...that 'he' thought was great
      summarizing some of the lies that he has told,
now he is seeking a parade...to honor 'him at this stage
      people of America, have our blood gone cold??

Impeachment is in the air...but he doesn't care
      he got the 'power' in his hand
he as gone all over the earth...making life for others worst
      because Trump is a very evil man.

Hargis
2/9/2018

SHOOTERS

It seems like every week...we hear about some creep
      that have killed a lot of people somewhere,
little children, women, and men...in schools, church, concerts there is
no end
      because the deranged can get guns and they don't care.

There are people that are carrying the load...who are ready to explode
      because 'profit' have put their life in a bind,
when you are living in the streets...and get enough to eat
      a hard life and seasons will keep you from crying.

There are those who understand...that 'money' is the God of this land
      and the pressure to keep going is sometimes hard to bare,
so with a gun and a twisted mind...it's just a matter of time
      until they show the world that they care.

About the injustice that is taking place...(the in-equality, the cost of living,
and mistreatment of religion and race)
      causing them to feel the pressure every minute of the day,
some try to seek help...but they don't have the wealth
      so they think shooting is the only way.

It doesn't look like it's going to change...with guns already in the hands
of the racist and the deranged
      safety in America is a hope and a prayer,
the President nor Congress won't push the issue...thinking it will stop
them from getting richer
      SO BE WARNED MY PEOPLE, SHOOTERS ARE
      EVERYWHERE.

Hargis
3/17/18

THE MOVEMENT
A NEW BEGINNING

The children of today...are challenging the NRA
      and the Government for 'gun' control,
too many killings in schools...cause there are no rules
      so the demented minds are bold.

They started a march...to express what's in their hearts
      but the politicians still won't give in,
the NRA money is so strong...they aren't concerned about right or wrong
      cause they know that 'money' is the God in men.

Countless of children have been shot and killed...the President is trying
to make a deal
      to show his loyalty to NRA,
he said the NRA is so dear...but everybody know that it something he fears
      and Congress just let him have his way.

Millions of children have come to DC...to give their insight to what
their future should be
      and demand safety in their class rooms,
raising the age is what some seek...but that won't stop the guns from
hitting the streets
      or the other shooting that are coming soon.

If a person with a gun is willing...no one can stop him from killing
      in America it's the mind set,
look at all of the unarmed Blacks that have died...by the police who
have lied
      and most have not been convicted yet.

They blame the shooting on the mental ill...and the back ground check deal
      but no one is looking at hatred and desire,
to put a gun in a teachers' hand...all across this land
      is like sitting in gasoline and playing with fire.

Some say that this issue will pass...and the children will go back to their class
     until the next shooting take place,
then parents will cry again...and politician will act like friends
     because 'lives' aren't important to NRA,

to the children of the world...I'm talking to the boys and the girls
     TV will make you think that you are doing good,
but ideology is what has to be changed...the rethinking in the brain
     so that nothing is misunderstood.

Hargis
3/24/18

TRUMP
(ALL BY HIMSELF)

Trump world is getting tight...thinking he can do what he likes
   because of his wealth,
and his position on the Hill...is giving the people a chill
   making decisions for the world all by himself.

His aids and lawyers are moving on...saying (in most cases) the President
is wrong
   his main concern is Trump,
he is a con-man from way back...talking about things without any facts
   but in reality he is just a rich chump.

A year and a half in...he has created a new trend
   tweeting about every thought in his head,
his people don't know what to say...some just turn and walk away
   and ignore the dis-respectful things said.

Personally, Trump don't give a shit...cause he think that he can handle
all of this
   but other leaders of the world think he is a fool,
he doesn't listen to any advise...he just open his mouth and roll the dices
   using his (so called) skills from the streets as his tool.

He denies everything he said...trying to fuck with your head
   with Sarah and Kellyann defending his lies,
when they talk to the press...they do their best
   in trying to make the President look 'wise'.

Mueller is on his ass...about Russia, his family, and his cash
   but Trump is lying at every turn,
he has this personal thing...and he uses his Office to be mean
   America, America when will we learn??

Lets not get it twisted...lets look at it realist ed
Trump has got the power in his hand,
like him or not...he can't be stopped
until the people rise up and take an impeachable stand.

Hargis
3/26/18

THE NEED
(FOR KNOWLEDGE AND UNDERSTANDING)

Some times you have to stop and take a deep breath...and thank GOD
if you have good health
     in a world where chemicals are king,
from the food that you eat...to the drugs that make you sleep
     chemicals will alter your thoughts and dreams.

Chemicals in food...is no new news
     but your body reactions is the thing,
everything you buy...is filled with some form of dye
     that will, also, affect your off springs.

In the Southern States...most people are over weight
     eating every part of that pig,
you know that the Jews just declared...that eating that pig is now fair
     modern day chemicals (this is big).

The people have lost control...over their health and their soul
     in America, deceit is a major tool,
Doctors are constantly lying...and people are steady dying
     experimenting with different drugs to use.

They used chemicals in Viet 'Num'...causing everyone some harm
     and the Government still won't tell the truth,
people are growing seven and eight feet tall...children are trying to walk
before they can crawl
     look how chemicals have affected our youth.

You know they are 'cloning' animals today...and people are their way
     but chemicals have slowed down any resistance,
technology as a whole is good...but when you add chemicals, things
get misunderstood
     there is a great need for a brand new system.

'The people must be free'

Hargis
4/7/18

THE DEVILS' RECEIPT

The news today is insane...the weather, the White House, the shootings,
and the sex scandals are the blame
      or has the devil 'doubled up'?
They say he is pissed cause Mueller crossed his line...and he is picking
off his staff one at a time
      the devil is still fighting cause he doesn't give a fuck.

Everywhere he goes he raises hell...he shouldn't be in the House he
should be in jail
      or under ground,
with his base by his side...they all should be fired
      and not be allowed to make 'human' sounds.

With Mueller, Russia, and miss Daniel too...the devil don't know what to do
      he wants to shoot his missiles and drop bombs,
he changes his mind every other day...his staff don't know what to say
      but the whole wold is watching and gathering their arms.

Paul Ryan gave it up...saying that the White House sucks
      and that there is no order to be found,
he used his kids as his out...but in reality it's the devils' mouth
      plus there is no solid ground.

Mike P. is looking confused...thinking that he might have to fill the
devils' shoes
      with no support from the Hill,
with 'war' knocking on the door...and the rich rippling off the poor
      he just wished that he had a stronger pills.

The devil is in his zone...and has Fox news saying he has done nothing wrong
      and that Mueller should leave,
the 'red necks' prayed for this drama...to get rid of Obama
      so now they are seeing shit they can't believe.

He is firing everyone who doesn't see it his way...taking their will and
their pay
  because the devil is on a mission,
white folks singed this contract with blood...it had nothing to do with
America love
  this is the receipt for destruction and he is the only cook in the
  kitchen.

Hargis
4/12/18

"THE TRUTH"
WILL IT SET YOU FREE?

It's time for mid-term elections...we'll get a chance to make another selection
      for our representative on Capital Hill,
there should be no confusion...about gun laws, sex, or Russian collusion
      our 'vote' has got to be for real.

We've got a President that's doing his own thing...destroying families,
and lives, and the American dream
      giving racism and hatred a different high,
if you are keeping up with the news...you'll see that he is surrounded
by fools
      that's doing nothing but justifying his lie.

Giuliani is a disgrace...on TV lying in the American face
      he and Trump are on the same page,
now Roseann has join the team...with statements that are mean
      causing some to say "it's an outrage".

Everybody wants to know when...will the impeachment begin?
      Or is Mueller just a part of Trumps' reality show?
History has taught us...that there are some people you just can't trust
      so America, America what do we really know?

The mentality that is in control...know that 'issues' are like gold
      they are designed to keep you confused,
they make good ratings for a show...even though
      people get hurt and mis-used.

"The people must be free"

Hargis
5/31/18

SOME OF US WOKE UP

Some of us woke up happy
some of us woke up mad
some of us woke up confused
      with their heart beating fast.

Some of us woke up with their blood pressure high
      and their sugar out of control
some of us woke up in very good health
      with love deep in their soul.

Some of us woke up in a nice soft bed
some of us woke up in the streets
some of woke up in a real bad mood
some of woke up with nothing to eat.

Some of us woke up behind prison walls
some of us woke up feeling totally free
some of us woke up thinking about their jobs
some of us woke up praying the 'she or he' let them be.

But we all woke up...life is what it is
and today your situation will bring about smiles or tears

"Tell your family that you love them...give them a hug or a kiss
and remember that God is in charge of the good and the bad of all of this"

Hargis
6/3/18

"L.A.M.P."
LAME ASS MALE PIMP

Time is moving fast...you can't let the dust settle on your ass
  because 'progress' made is fading away,
slavery tactics are now been used...separation of family is the new border rule
  and the A G used the bible to justify this day.

The shit Trump is doing...is justification for suing
  but Congress is afraid to make a move,
Trump is hustling Capital Hill...using fear to make his deal
  causing the manhood of America to be screwed.

Tramp is running his game...challenging the Democrats with no shame
  trying to get them to publicly react,
on the streets(out west) this used to be called 'lamp'...
to get other Pimps and Hustlers to expose their camp
  but it's an act of fear because it has no facts.

Rudy, Sarah, and the AG are doing their part...to misinform the people,
keeping them in the dark
  and confused about all of Trumps' lies,
the (old) Hustlers are saying "dam...no one can see his scheme"?
  but Congress is operating with closed eyes.

Coming to America seeking hope...life in their country ain't no joke
  thinking Democracy is great,
but finding out a new truth...as this Government take away their youth
  expressing to the world, tremendous hate.

What about the 'American Dream'...love, peace, and nice material things
  all of that Trump is trying to still,
he doesn't care about wrong or right...times in America is tight
  except for those who are trying to make a deal.

Hargis
6/18/18

108

EVERYBODY IS WAITING TO SEE

It's the 27th of July...the American people are wondering why
    that Trump is not in jail,
with with all of the corruption he has done...with his layers and his son
    the justice system has failed.

MSNBC...has it all on TV
    but Mueller seem to be taking his time,
Trump said that he is the target of hate...but they have it all on tape
    he has committed crime after crime after crime.

Everywhere Trump turns...there is fire waiting to burn
    his ass and his supporters too,
it seems like Sarah wants to quit...cause she is tired of all this shit
    trying to make lies sound like the truth.

All over the world...Trump has unfurled
    the evil that's in his soul,
then he calls it a 'good' thang...and coming before the people with no shame
    but everything is beginning to unfold.

We know that God is just...in him we have to keep our trust
    he said that "every eye will see",
the number on his forehead and in his hand...before they take a stand
    then man can go back to being free.

But until that time...Trump is fucking with everybody's mind
    because he wants to dictate,
but he is in for a shock...when the hammer is dropped
    then he will realize that it's him and not the news that fake.

Russia, China, Korea, and Japan...Canada, Mexico, UK, and the motherland
    all trying to make sense of the things he say,
he has his own set of rules...cause he think everyone is a fool
    and that they should thank God for him when they pray.

His day is coming and it won't be long...he will realize that he is all along
he will still cry 'fake news' and the lousy press
he will still blame Hillary and Obama for all of his mess.

He'll still think that he's the greatest President that ever lived
and all of his accomplishments that he never fulfilled.

One day they will find him in an alley face down on the ground…
or in a mental ward wearing a slip and a gown.

For now, Trump is the man...with no master plan
      he is filled with destruction and hate,
his party is beginning to understand...and distance themselves from this man
      because they know that their political lives are at stake.

Hargis
7/27/18

DO WHAT WE MUST

It's happening again and again...the killing of Black men
    in many cities in most States,
our families get too excited...when on one is indicted
    the grand jury and the lawyers are filled with racial hate.

The Black man...after 600 years in this land
    is still uneducated and misused,
some have become famous and rich...house niggas and the white man's bitch
    and for a few dollars will become his fool.

We are still trying to over come one thing or another...following in the
foot steps of our fathers and our mothers
    but still they shoot us down and the courts let them go,
no laws have been changed...it is us who are the blame
    cause we dress up to march and sing and put on a show.

Now lets not get it twisted...these shooters are sadistic
    but 'we' have no plans to change the law,
we depend on the ones' who pull the trigger...the same ones that still
call us nigger
    and the very same ones that we call boss.

There was a woman who made a deal...her actions got Emmett Till killed
    but years later, she said she lied,
keeping up with the flow...the court and the State let it go
    cause Black people don't have any pride.

With the talent we have and the money we make...Black people (organized)
can really be great
    and demand respect from the mentality of this land,
we must do unto others as they do unto us...and take whatever course
that we must
    cause our future and our survival depends on the Black man.

Hargis
7/29/18

THE PICTURE IS GETTING CLEARER

The President of America is now center stage...his wife and his daughter
say he is an outrage
      he just open his mouth and out come shit,
that's nothing new I suppose...but what else do you expect from an ass hole
      impeachment is the only thing that will fit.

Some of his supporters are beginning to break away...
cause of the things he is doing and the things he say.

His cabinet took a stand and express themselves with affection...
letting the people know that the Russians did tamper with the 2016 election.

At the same time he was telling a crowd that the tampering wasn't real...
and that the Mueller investigation should be killed.

He had promised to build a wall and that Mexico would pay
now he wants to shut down the Government until he gets the money
from the USA.

Now he is really upset...cause Mueller is looking into his debts
      and the deals he made over a period of time,
he is tweeting hard and fast...after Mueller's ass
      cause Mueller got proof of all of his crimes.

Within the family there seems to be a little distrust...
so Trump is trying to throw his son under the bus.

He has kidnapped Mexican children with a policy of his own...
defied a court order because he never thinks that he is wrong.

He has started a Tariff war with other Country thinking things will be cheaper…
now he is shouting to the world that the 'press' is the <u>enemy</u> <u>of</u> <u>the</u> <u>people</u>.

Trump is the 'devil' in human form
America, America you have been warned.

Hargis
8/5/18

"FADING"

Well now it's finally been said...that Trump got a serious problem in his head
>   but many knew this from the start,
he hustled up some votes...squeezing many by the throat
>   and taking from his party members, their hearts.

Still they try to explain his lies...but some are beginning to open their eyes
>   DONALD TRUMP IS NO JOKE,
he has given out signs...of his state of mind
>   now he is threatening to sink the whole boat.

America, today, is been robbed...because Congress won't do their job
>   and remove him from his seat,
they all know that he is not right...but they continue to fight
>   hoping that the President will pass out some political treats.

There will be a race war soon...cause hatred is filling up the room
>   and we know that a house divided can not stand,
America will cry...cause many will die
>   in every City and in every State across this land.

These are dangerous times in our home...while other Countries are looking on
>   trying to find weakness or strength,
Russia, China, and Korea...are sitting back in the rear
>   because they know that Trump is not making any sense.

America democracy is on its' sick bed...with no IV and a pillow on her head
>   crying out to the people for aid,
but if Congress do not intervene...and be a part of the life saving team
>   America as we know it will fade.

Hargis
8/8/18

A GOOD-BY KISS

There are fires on the west coast
heat in the mid–west
rain and hail on the east coast
the south has been blessed.

God is upset...cause we are not doing our best
    to make this planet safe,
those with the know...won't let that knowledge flow
    but God 'will' turn this land into a waste.

As he has done many times in the past...God will destroy our ass
    but God is just,
you may be a master in that stock...or shooting that rock
    but caring for one another is a must.

It's not just the Presidents or Kings...Dictators or Queens
    it's a global concern,
mercy will be spared for some...the worst is yet to come
    but 95% will burn.

This is in 'your' book that you call good...which is mis-understood
    because wrong is right and right is wrong,
evil is pushing life very fast...and got us worshiping cash
    marching and singing songs.

I'm just telling the tale...about our earthly hell
    and all the chances that we have missed,
so sit back and relax...because this destruction is a fact
    just tell your ass good–by and give it a kiss.

Hargis
8/8/18

BY THE COLOR OF YOUR SKIN

Civil war is just about here...a lot of people are living in fear
> because of the color of their skin,
the President is instigating a violent fight...between the Brown, Black, and White
> a war that no one can win.

Racism is a part of our history...so the rules of this war(to us)won't be no mystery
> but this is 2018,
some Blacks and Whites...are really tight
> this will impede their American dream.

Some Whites think they are in charge...of the environment at large
> some even think they are God,
it's because their DNA is so 'weak'...they are filled hatred and malady
> and the President has given them the nod.

To their surprise...love and common sense is on the rise
> "make America white" is the racist cry,
the Skin Heads and the Klan...try hard to put fear in every man
> but those are the days gone by.

They gave the Black woman 'the pill'...so her un-born babies would be killed
> they felt that the Black race was growing too fast,
they had it (back then) in their mind...about this day and time
> when the Black man will rise up from the trash.

They have been trying to control our birth...all over the planet earth
> for hundreds of years,
they used hanging, bombing, and beat us raw...jobs, schools and government law
> they changed our names, our language, our religion, and our fears.

There are some Whites who are in the know...about this racial show
   and all of the historical facts,
that 'man' and 'man kind' is not the same...and Jesus had a Muslim name
   and the God you worship is Black.

Black leadership is not interested in Black health...only in their own wealth
   they talk tough but are looking for donations,
white supremacy don't give a shit...weather you are pure Black or mixed
   their goal is white liberation.

Some of you think that you are in control...but this 'hate thing' will
take your soul
   and have you talking about "issues to mend",
this race war is going to be tight...and every man, woman, and child is
gonna have to fight
   because this war will be about the color of your skin.

Hargis
8/10/18

VOTING
(NOVEMBER 2018)

Mid-term election has come and gone...the smooth talking politicians
are back in their home
    leaving our community with nothing at all,
didn't nothing change...but we all should know this game
    the promises, the lies, and the meetings in town halls.

There are still pot holes in the streets...our 'old people' are still getting beat
    carjackings and break-Ins are everywhere,
mass killings are still taking place...police are still killing (depending
on your race)
    and the homeless population is still growing, cause no one cares.

Republicans and Democrats are all in the same boat.....white and black
faces in the hood handing out 'hope'
    to get our 'mark' at the voting booth,
but what can they do?...what can they really do for me and you?
    Outside of winding us up and turning us loose.

America has a President that is completely insane...do and say what he
wants and have no shame
    he has made other politicians death and blind,
any news against him is fake...but he tells everyone that he is great
    and nothing that he does is a crime.

Most are hoping for changes on Capital Hill...and that the President
will take some deep breaths and chill
    and stop telling Americas that they are the blame,
but the reality is that he'll never quit...and he strikes back at anyone
who challenges his shit
    like I said, this President is insane.

Currently there are re-counts all over the land...(the bible said the mark is in his forehead and in his hand)

but 'voting' is not going to set any one free,
we have to come together...and fight the 'illness' of this weather
from sea to shining sea.

Hargis
11-13-18

EXPECTATION

Expectation Expectation...is rooted in all of Gods creations
    because everything in life is connected,
when you are torn from your mothers womb...you are expected to cry soon
    so your mother won't think that you are defected.

You expect relationships to be healthy and fine
You are expected to understand why your lady is crying
You expect teachers to teach and preachers to preach
You expect what they say is good
You expect their help in developing the hood
You expect the water you drink to be safe
You don't expect mistreatment because of the color of face
You expect safe and affordable houses to live in
You expect respect from all of your so-called friends
You expect your mother and father to understand
You expect family to lend a helping hand
You expect love from those to whom you give love
You expect answers to your prayer from the God up above
You expect the food that you eat be safe and clean
You expect a good night sleep and a beautiful dream
You expect the people next door to friendly and polite
You expect to live in a community where you can walk the streets at night

Sometimes your expectations may change over night...and because of
that change
Sometimes you may have to fight.

"free your mind and your ass will follow"

Hargis
11-16-18

"WHAT DO YOU THINK?"

As we head toward the end of the year...Trump has his party dressed in fear
      pimping like the mob out of the white house,
he say and do things that ain't right...he got his party members wrapped up tight
      they all act like a frighten mouse.

Kelly and the boys say that Trump is great...and that his racist bull shit is not hate
      he is just miss-understood,
this impeachment will make you see...that the US President he shouldn't be
      I've never seen a 'Presidential Poll' in the hood.

Trump is a hustler from way back...a crook, a theft, and a hater of blacks
      but dumb poor 'red necks' love him to death,
he was called from down below...to spead his evil everywhere he go
      uprooting stability and destroying people health.

I vote for impeachment and remove him from this land...Trump is the devil and he is a danger to every woman and every man
      his bull shit around the world has been plenty,
don't get me wrong...his supporters are strong
      so we all need to vote him out in 2020.

"If you free you mind, you ass will follow"

Hargis
11/16/19

"CORONA"
A NEW KID ON THE BLOCK

2020...a year that got plenty
    of people dying,
from a deadly decease...you catch from a cough or a sneeze
    and a President on 'TV' everyday lying.

The people was ordered to stay in...no more hand shakes with love ones
or friends
    because there is no cure in sight,
everything is closed...business and hoes
    trains, buses, and flights.

Corona is her name...and she has no shame
    taking down millions pretty fast,
there were some that got brave...who are now in their grave
    they refused to wear gloves and masks.

The President threw out some money...and lied about 'Corona' will be
gone when it sonny
    then encouraged the people to fuck the in house order,
he wants to open up stores...to the delight of streets whores
    but "corona' is kicking ass from border to border.

It ain't just in the US...other Countries are in the same mess
    the scientists of the world are working hard,
but on one can find a drug...that can close the gates to this flood
    now doctors are saying "this is only the start".

The economy in America is really hurt...over 30 millions people are
out of work
    Congress approved a 3.3 trillion dollar bill,
millions went to the rich...they claimed it was a system glick
    but most of them kept that money still.

It was designed to keep small business afloat...but now they have no hope
    of recovering from this shout down,
a lot of banks wouldn't help black business at all...hoping that their
business will fall
        now black business are waiting for another stimulus around.

Hargis
5/16/20

THE LIE ABOUT THE LIE

Trump is telling lies...because black people are on the rise
      voting and demanding that he be removed,
Americas' morals are down the drain...people of authority have no shame
      Trump has convinced many he didn't lose.

The republicans and democrats are at war...democracy has been striped
so far
      power is their goal,
"dame the people", they say...look like politicians have lost their way
      not giving a shit if democracy fold.

Trump followers don't understand...the deep seeded evil of this man
      and the things he is willing to do,
he will throw his friends under the bus...his children he will crush
      and bring out all of the hatred in you.

He has the control of many minds...they think he is doing fine
      and he is great in their eye sight,
he has asked lawyers and congressmen to lie...he wants to be President
until he die
      for him they are willing to fight.

Impeached twice but the Senate let him go...I think Mitch McConnell
is his hoe
      other republicans are spreading their cheeks wide,
those who say 'no'...the party say you have got to go
      a few won't 'man up' they just hide.

His followers can't do the math...or his lie won't last
      so he want to pull a coup,
to get reinstalled...you are talking about big balls
      Trump has some democrats jumping through hoops.

The 'Big Lie' is about the election...that has some States trying to make corrections

by recounting all the votes,

what ever happened to 'the law' of the land...why can't Congress and the court stop this man?

Look like Trump is more powerful than dope.

Hargis
4-19-21

IN THE SENATE??

I was watching the news...and heard Trump call some of the Senators 'fools'
>   because they voted to help President Biden make life better for
>   the people,
Trump, also, called them losers and weak...but loyalty to him, most will still keep
>   hatred in his heart seem to be deep.

What he doesn't understand...is that democracy is bigger than one man
>   he really can't see be young himself,
he had his shot...but 'organized' he was not
>   he only saw things through the eyes of wealth.

He is talking about running for the 'house' again...he knows nothing now and he knew nothing then
>   dictatorship is what he seeks,
he thinks that the country is his toy...and misinformation and confusion gives him joy
>   he thinks that the American people are weak.

He just make up stuff as he go...and Mitch McConnell (his ho)
>   will justify and spread the shit,
sometimes Trump gets mad...and publicly spank his ass
>   but Mitch knows that he is Trump's bitch.

McConnell did vote for President Biden's bill...every was shocked on the Hill
>   the bill will help create jobs everywhere,
nineteen Republicans said yes...the American people were impressed
>   finally, some good news from Washington we can share.

Hargis
8-2-21

SANITY CHECK

We are living in historical times...some of this shit will blow your mind
     when looking at the reality of today,
this virus is still killing...Trump still ain't willing
     to admit he lost, cause he wants to stay.

In Jan., Trump people stormed the 'hill'...trying to over throw the
election and the Vise President to kill
     all because Trump didn't like the deal,
he started early in the year..implanting in his followers minds 'fear'
     and that the only he could loose is a steal.

Biden won fair and square...but Trump don't care
     he has unlocked the evil in millions of minds,
he said the election was wrong...and he had to give up his home
     now he is traveling all over the country lying.

Other Republicans have joined in...saying Trump did win
     now they are trying to pass new voting laws,
because the 'black' votes were so strong...Trump wants to keep them
at home
     in order to destroy the democracy walls.

Trump walks around with his head up high...because he has convinced
millions of the "big lie"
     they really think that the election will change,
Congress is beginning to look at the 'insurrection' that took place on
the sixth
some Republicans are saying that it didn't exist
     and Trump shouldn't be the blame.

Doj is looking at all the things that Trump did...but Trump is trying to close the lid

  by diverting the public minds,

American people you have got to be strong...what Trump did and is doing is wrong

  and he should be jailed for all of his crimes.

Hargis
7-28-21

AMERICA
GOD IS PRESENT
CAN'T YOU SEE?

Heat waves, storms, and fires...covid19, deaths, and cries
 America today is been torn apart,
the 45th keep turning up the heat...like a child, he can't take defeat
 evil and darkness is in his heart.

Some Governors out of their ugliness won't mandate masks...so people in every state are dying fast
 parents are suing over this situation,
the health of our children are at stake...Governors are signing order without any debates
 they have cut off all community relations.

Some are talking about not paying schools...that defy their orders and break the rules
 even though children are getting sick and dying,
there is 'civil war' that's taking place...alone with the out cries of hate and race
 all of this because the 'devil' is lying.

Mis-information is their weapon of choice...the Republicans are passing laws so that some people will have no voice
 mainly people with black and brown skin,
a few State Senators have been jailed...for trying to DE-rail
 these evil acts and voting sins.

In many states this evil is taking affect...so that the devil can have an unfair chance for re-elect
 in the year 2024,

but make no mistake...even though he is pushing hate
God and the American people will close that door.

"America, America, the truth will set you free
If you would open up your mind so your eyes can see".

Hargis
8-19-21

YESTERDAY IS TODAY

We were brought to this land...enslaved by the white man
      through trickery and brutal force,
we were raped and killed...surviving on nothing but our will
      now today they show no remorse.

The Constitution had laws...that stated 'we weren't full humans at all'
      so it was 'OK' to do all those things,
they took our homes and raped our wives...burned down our communities
took our lives
      and ignored through out history our cries and screams.

All of the land lords owned slaves...it made their children brave
      to carry on their brutal attacks,
the courts "said the white man can't be blamed"...and today they are
saying the same
      even though there are video showing the facts.

80 years ago, we start marching and signing songs...letting the world
know that our killing was wrong
      but no justice did we receive,
this country mentality has not changed...and the laws of the land is still
the same
      so we just cry and grieve.

There are some that say that life is getting better...and that 'black lives'
matter
      but the killings have not stopped,
there is still no justice for most...because we depend on the host
      just like yesterday they're feeding us 'slop'.

Some of us got money, degrees, and think we are wise...we justice our
existence but won't organize
          afraid of losing our 'spot',
while most of us are living in poverty and shame...now society say "that
we only have ourselves to blame"
          just like yesterday, we continue to eat the 'slop'.
Yesterday is today and our killings ain't right...only today we're killing
each other along with the whites
          because this country teaches everyone to hate,
we are constantly being put to the test...but all we do is march and protest
          and sometimes we sit down and deliberate

The grand jury still say no...so justice can't flow
          to our grieving families in need,
so today we may get pissed...but this country mentality still existence
          mistreatment, destruction, and greed.

Hargis
8-29-21

IT' HARD TO BREAK

What sense does it make...when all around you is hate
    church, schools, police, and so-called friends,
nothing happen if you pray...this virus won't go away
    it seems that everyone heart is filled with sin.

Thousands people are still getting sick...Governors in some States don't give a shit
    they got this 'us vs them' mentality,
they won't mandate schools to wear masks...even after some of the kids passed
    they are over looking 'reality'.

Trump is the root cause...he knows that his party don't have the balls
    to break his grip,
a few went astray...to vote President Biden's way
    but now they have tighten up their lips.

20 years of fighting in Afghanistan...President Biden took a stand
    and brought the troops back home,
some Republicans got mad...and tried to crucify his ass
    by saying "ending the war was wrong".

Thousands of Americans are dead...after spending two trillion of America's 'bread'
    most Americans are glad,
there are those who still spread lies...who are not and won't be satisfied
    to them, every decision by President Biden is bad.

<u>"When your mind and heart is filled with hate"</u>
<u>"That's a hard mentality to break"</u>

This virus and hurricanes...mass killings and climate change
        and fires burning out of control,
some people can hardly breadth or eat...drinking the contaminated
water or take a leak
        now they are restricting voting at the poles.

Hospitals are over crowded and have no beds...still many won't take the
shots and end up dead

Some people are sleeping in shelters...some are sleeping in the streets
some people can't change clothes and have no shoes on their feet.

Some people lost their homes, can't afford the note
unemployment ran out, they are just broke.

President Biden introduced a bill that will ease the suffering and pain
but Mitch and his boys said "no...we're going to stop his show"
        they are willing to let people die,
this mentality is hard to break...because their mjnds and hearts are filled
with hate
        all because Trump created the big lie.

"Free your mind and your ass will follow"

Hargis
9-1-21

CAN THEY BE STOPPED??

The Republicans are at it again...stopping abortion because killing is a sin.

It's not like letting people starve to death...because the rich won't share their wealth.

Or mandate the mask safety rule...to keep kids from dying in schools.

In Texas, a reward is paid...against anyone who gives aid
     to a pregnant woman seeking an abortion pass six weeks,
now everyone is on alert...not caring who they hurt
     because it's that money they seek.

A woman has the right..and shouldn't have to fight
     about giving birth,
but Republicans seem to thank...they can pull rank
     to determine when and who can or can not come onto this earth.

The Republicans plan is as plain as day...bring about confusion any how any way
     by bringing forth issues after issues,
the Democrats are taking their time...not letting the Republicans blow their minds
     working to make their bills official.

The Republican States are passing laws that are really mean...and the Supreme Court
won't inter vein
     so the American people will suffer and some will die,
you can't blame the virus when you are displaying hate...
you have to blame the Senators that represent your State
     because they are the ones who are spreading 'the big lie'.

Hargis
9-3-21

"DIRT"
THE FINAL COVER UP

Grave yards are running out of plots...cause people won't wear masks or get the shots

    trying to up hold some bull shit information,
they don't trust the Government or the science...they don't trust their eyes or their ears when they see and hear people dying

    but they love to talk about our great nation.

This virus has got us by the throat...and still Republicans won't vote

    to allow the President to give aid,
some Senators are firm in their belief...and don't give a shit about the people relief

    as long as they get paid.

Some Senators and Governors need to be replaced...for their mistreatment of the human race

    and allowing this virus to do as it please,
babies and children are dying right before their eyes...because they believe all of Trump's lies

    and his deep rooted hatred needs.

Fox news has drawn the line...and reported that Trump has committed 'no' crimes

    even though millions of American breath no more,
Congress and DA(s) are conducting investigations...on Trump's attempt to destroy our nation

    his actions can no longer be ignored.

Recount audits are proving that nothing was wrong...but Trump and the Republicans are still singing that same old song

    about his election lost,
still many believe that Trump is right...and are willing to keep up the fight

    to them, Trump is still the boss.

So what can we do...I'm talking about me and you
and all who have been hurt?
between this virus, Congress, and the weather...we have got to get our
shit together
or they will be covering us up with 'dirt'.

Hargis
10-1_2

'ONE DAY WE WILL'

One day we will look back and see.. what really happened in history
      the virus, the transformation, the big lie,
we will come to know...how evil took over the show
      and his efforts to get Democracy to die.

We all saw the insurrection on Capital Hill...directed by Trump to stop
the so called 'steal'
      his people went full speed ahead,
he brought out of them, their hatred and fire...when he created the <u>stop
the steal lie</u>
      it left many hurt and many dead.

It's not funny...but evil hit the floor running
      setting up shop everywhere he went,
he convinced most...that he was the perfect host
      his first task was to destroy the previous President.

History will show that for five years...how he unleashed his evil fears
      all over the planet earth,
in some states, he had demons waiting at the top...and when he gave
orders (most) Americans were shocked
      then he washed away their humanity, to give evil his birth.

One day we will look back and see...what really happened in history
      that caused the Supreme Court to turn the other cheek,
and allow some states...to practice hate
      that will keep the people weak.

Until then, we have to fight for Democracy rights...and understand that in unity there is might

because evil is moving faster than our since of time,
he has taken over one party...and destroyed their order
now 'his will' is in their mind.

Yes, one day we will look back and see...what really happened in history when "WE THE PEOPLE" thought that we were free.

Hargis
10/29/21

ABOUT THE AUTHOR

I was born in the spring of 1949 in Chattanooga, TN. I attended Howard High School where I played basketball, which allowed me to attend college (with the aid of a basketball scholarship). I joined the military (Navy) in 1968 and was honorable discharged in 1974. The military allotted me many benefits. It allowed me to see, visit and experience many countries on this earth. It, also, allowed me to resume my college education. My discipline was business administration with accounting and bookkeeping I worked in that field for over twenty years before returning to Chattanooga in 1993 where I worked with mentally and physically challenged people until I retired in 2017.

My poetic inspiration was presented to me in 1966 by a poetic group called 'The Last Poets'.

I started writing about my relationship with America in 1968. And today 53 years later, I am still writing about my relationship with America (the place I love so dear)